MILLION FAMILY MARCH

THE

NATIONAL

AGENDA

PUBLIC POLICY ISSUES, ANALYSES,
AND PROGRAMMATIC PLAN OF ACTION

2000–2008

Million Family March
145 Kennedy Street, NW
Washington, D.C. 20011

On September 27, 1996, at the conclusion of the National Political
Convention held in St. Louis, Missouri, sponsored by the National African
American Leadership Summit (NAALS) and the Million Man March, Inc. as a
follow-up to the October 16, 1995, Million Man March in Washington, D.C.,
*THE NATIONAL AGENDA: U.S. Public Policy Issues and Action Items for
1996–2000* was ratified and published.

As a result of the call of the Honorable Minister Louis Farrakhan for the
Million Family March, October 16, 2000, in Washington, D.C., the current draft
of *THE NATIONAL AGENDA: Public Policy Issues, Analyses, and
Programmatic Plan of Action 2000–2008* reflects the broadening of outreach
to be inclusive of the entire human family.

Contents

SECTION 1
FAMILY, MORALITY, AND PUBLIC POLICY

SECTION 2
POLITICAL EMPOWERMENT

SECTION 3
JUSTICE ISSUES

SECTION 4
STRENGTHENING THE FAMILY

SECTION 5
QUALITY OF LIFE

SECTION 6
ECONOMIC TRANSFORMATION

SECTION 7
INTERNATIONAL AFFAIRS

Foreword

"Why Should There Be A National Agenda?"[1]

It is clear from watching the political debate that has been going on in the country for the last several years that there is and has been a steady erosion of the principles of democracy. If this is to be a government of the people, by the people, and for the people, then the enlightenment of the people must be the cornerstone of a truly democratic society. It is only when the masses of the people are enlightened and have an enlightened self-interest that their vote in a democratic society has real meaning. With the erosion of the American educational system and the graduating of young people out of high school of whom 30 percent are considered functionally illiterate; with the dumbing down of the American people that they become as sheep, easily led in the wrong direction, easily manipulated by powerful forces, then, democracy begins to lose its meaning in the lives of the masses of the American people; producing a tremendous degree of dissatisfaction. As a result, there has been a continuous decline in voter-turnout and participation in the last few presidential elections.

In the last presidential election, according to what we understand, nearly 50 percent of those eligible to vote actually participated in the electoral process. This means that one-half of the electorate did not bother to vote in the last presidential election. So, President Clinton won the election with nearly 30% of the 50% of the people who did vote which means that approximately 70% of the American people did not vote for President Clinton. The rise of anti-government sentiment reflected in the militia and in other organizations and groups within the country, and with mass dissatisfaction being seen among the people–Black, White, Hispanic, Asian and Pacific Islander, and Arab---are signs that the wise should and must reflect upon.

In the last few years corporate America has spent nearly a billion dollars a year through their Washington lobbyists to enact legislation that is in the best interest of corporate America, while not necessarily in the best interest of the masses of the American people. Corporate America is now buying up newspapers, radio and television stations to control the means of dissemination of information to the American people. This is a further erosion of the principle of governance of, by, and for the people.

We will find increasingly that corporations and their strong lobbies drive America's foreign policy which the American people believe is in the

1. *Statement from The Honorable Minister Louis Farrakhan, Convener of the Million Family March and The National Representative of The Most Honorable Elijah Muhammad, January 4, 2000.*

THE NATIONAL AGENDA

best interest of the American people while in many instances these policies are "anti" the best interest of the American people.

The industrial base of this nation is steadily disappearing. It appears that manufacturing, which is the bedrock of the workforce in an industrial society, is being ceded to other countries in the name of free-market, economy and globalism - leaving the unlearned masses losing jobs and trying to fit in a service-orientated society. At some point, if the American people are not awakened they will wake up to find themselves under authoritarian, dictatorial rule masquerading itself as a democracy. Therefore, an agenda that comes from the people that is in the best interest of the people must be crafted so that the people are empowered to take the country back from the greedy merchants of death who now hold sway over the American government and its people. We have invited scholars from the various communities to give their input to an agenda that we believe can become the basis of legislation that helps to redistribute the tax dollars of the citizenry in a way that is much more beneficial.

This is the way that tax dollars can be redistributed:

- The greatest need of the American people is educational enlightenment. This is what brings the potential human being out of the animalistic stage into the existence of a human being with respect for moral law and the principle that allows human interaction in a way that is pleasing to God and pleasing to man.
- The next greatest need is the health of the people. Teaching the people the best way to eat to live and crafting those institutions that research, develop and explore new ways and means of curing disease.
- The most important need is that the country must be able to protect its citizenry through an enlightened, strong military force.

Each life is born into this universe with the responsibility and natural duty to do something for its self, otherwise it cannot justify its existence. All living creatures must do for self and it is this aspect of the natural law that the poorer class of American people, particularly Blacks, must accept their natural responsibility to get up, unite, and pool their resources and do everything that they can to develop themselves, create institutions that serve their needs and make government responsible to create the atmosphere that will allow all of the citizenry to enjoy the principles of freedom, justice and equality. These principles are the essential principles of life. The denial of any one of these is the denial of life itself. If the Founding Fathers saw that life, liberty and the pursuit of happiness are the inalienable rights of every citizen, then, we must maximize our ability to give life, liberty and the pursuit of happiness to ourselves and not just sit down and wait on benevolent government to do these things for us, for, the government is no longer now the true servant of the masses of the people, but has become the servant of those who are buying its votes and its allegiance in the name of democracy. This is why there must be a national agenda by the people, of the people, and for the people. This is why the national body must be enlightened so that we will make proper choices as to who will lead us and help to create a future for us and our children.

In a predominantly Judeo-Christian society, the Bible is or should be the basic book of instruction and guidance for the politicians as well as the people. The Bible begins with the Book of Genesis that tells us the story of creation. According to the Bible it was on the sixth day that God created man and woman. Before the creation of man and woman an entire earth and universe was created to serve the man and woman that God had created. So, the Bible teaches us that man, and it should be understood that this means man and woman, is The Glory of God. No matter how great all of creation is, the human being is the greatest of God's creation. The second act of creation on the sixth day was a female and God put these two together and gave them instructions. So, before there were nations, governments and systems there was family. This teaches us that the family is more important than the government and more important than the nation for it is out of family, and the needs of family, and the rights of family that governments are instituted among men.

The Holy Qur'an states the same principle differently. It teaches us that everything that God created was created to serve the human being. The importance of family and its preservation is the duty of all legitimate governments and systems. Anything that disrupts family or is against the general welfare of the family, is therefore against the aim and purpose of God and creation for He made all of creation to serve the man, the woman, the family.

Therefore, anything that we say or do that is not in the best interest of family, that injures family, must be revisited and changed. Everything that we say and do must promote the good of marriage, the good of family, and the development of family, then, we know that we are in accord with the aim and purpose of God in creating family.

I have stated that every human need is a basic human right and any denial of the basic needs of the human being is a denial of their basic human rights. The need of every human being physically is food, clothing and shelter. God has prepared the earth to provide the needs of all its creatures. Surely the greatest of God's creation, the human being, should have access to food, clothing and shelter.

The human being has a need to be loved and that love is the nurturing force of the life in that human being. Therefore, every human being has the need for nurturing. Therefore, there is a need for a mother, a need for a father, and the need for a family as the basic institution for the nurturing of the values that make us human beings.

In order that the human being be separated from the beast of the field there must be the introduction of knowledge and moral consciousness. Since the human being is created a social being, then there must be rules and regulations that govern human behavior that allow for good social relationships. This also is a human need and therefore a human right to grow up in an environment of love. Education is a human need. Therefore, it is a human right. Good government has the responsibility to ensure that its citizenry is properly educated.

Moral consciousness develops out of the values taught by parents and exemplified in the actions of parents so that the home becomes the nurturing ground for moral values and moral consciousness. All of this starts in the family. Since the country today is mired down with increase in violence, crime, child abuse, the abuse of women, then this is a manifestation of the imbalance of the human mind and this is a justification for a greater demand for proper education of all the citizens. When properly educated, properly nurtured, then all anti-social elements in behavior can be drastically eliminated.

The Honorable Minister Louis Farrakhan
National Representative of The Most Honorable Elijah Muhammad
and the Nation of Islam

Introduction

Where We Are After The Million Man March
Toward The Million Family March:

THE NATIONAL AGENDA 2000-2008

We are thankful to God for THE NATIONAL AGENDA 2000-2008. On behalf of the Million Family March, we are pleased to present this document to our people and constituencies across the United States of America and throughout the world.

We were all blessed when God worked through the Honorable Minister Louis Farrakhan to call for the Million Man March in 1995 and the present call for the Million Family March in 2000. Today and henceforth, we should take the necessary steps to continue to advance our interests toward atonement, reconciliation, responsibility, freedom, justice and equality.

THE NATIONAL AGENDA 2000-2008 is the result of gathering the input of tens of thousands of our people who are engaged in the day-to-day struggle on the local, regional, national and international levels. This input was then translated into policy recommendations with accompanying action recommendations.

We do not intend to allow our interests to be ignored or sacrificed during the current national political debate. While our initial focus in 1995 was on the plight and condition of African Americans, THE NATIONAL AGENDA 2000-2008 has been broadened to be inclusive of the issues and public policies that coincide with the interests of Hispanic Americans, Native Americans, Asian and Pacific Islanders, Arab Americans and White Americans, as well as others who have been marginalized.

Substantial information quoted and referenced in this document was edited directly from the Congressional Black Caucus (CBC), Congressional Hispanic Caucus (CHC), Leadership Conference on Civil Rights (LCCR), National Association for the Advancement of Colored People (NAACP), Urban League, National Association of Black Social Workers (NABSW) and the Joint Center for Political and Economic Studies (JCPES).

On October 16, 1995, the eyes of the world focused on more than one million Black men and others who traveled from all over America to assemble at the United States Capitol in Washington, D.C. Those who were present and the millions who witnessed this event through satellite television cannot properly put into words the power of that moment in world history. While there have been numerous debates about the purpose of the Million Man March convened by the Honorable Minister Louis Farrakhan and the accomplishments of those who attended, there is one fact upon which there is no ambiguity or confusion. The image of the Black man in America was changed from that moment forward. The image that was distributed around the world of Black men and Black people as buffoons, savages, criminals and menaces to society was challenged and changed forever.

The spirit of the Million Man March is the spirit of God and we were made to see that it is possible to take a greater responsibility to improve the quality of life of our families and communities. Many in the world community have tapped into this spirit and made the commitment that their communities will not be doomed to failure and despair as we begin the twenty first century. The Million Man March Mission Statement pledged:

> *The Million Man March and Day of Absence can only have lasting value if we continue to work and struggle beyond this day. Thus, our challenge is to take the spirit of this day, the process of mobilization and the possibilities of organization and turn them into ongoing structures and practices directed toward our liberation and flourishing as a people.[2]*

Thirty days after the Million Man March, on November 16, 1995, delegates from throughout the United States gathered on the campus of Howard University in Washington, D.C. for a meeting of the National African American Leadership Summit. The Leadership Summit adopted a Ten-Point Action Program that in part called for a National Political Convention to be held in 1996.

As a follow-up to the historic success of the Million Man March, the National Hearing on Issues and Public Policy, held on the campus of Kennedy-King College, Chicago, Illinois, July 26-27, 1996, produced *The National Agenda 1996: Executive Summary.*

The National Hearing on Issues and Public Policy served to facilitate a formal and systematic drafting of an outline of the most crucial concerns impacting the quality of life. We are grateful to those representatives and delegates who went to Chicago and participated fully in the national hearings.

In September 1996, the National Political Convention was convened in St. Louis, Missouri. The Convention was attended by thousands of delegates from throughout the United States. The National African American Leadership Summit (NAALS) and The Million Man March, Inc. co-sponsored the convention. The two major results of the convention were the adoption of a document entitled *The National Agenda: Public Policy Issues and Action Items 1996-2001;* and, the tremendous increase in voter-turnout in the 1996 national elections, particularly among Black men. The Joint Center for Political and Economic Studies based in Washington, D.C. documented the unprecedented upsurge in Black male voting in the national elections in

2.   The Million Man March/Day of Absence Mission Statement: Dr. Maulana Karenga and the Executive Council of the National Million Man March/Day of Absence Organizing Committee, *Washington, D.C., October 16, 1995, p. 17.*

November 1996. Of course, the increase of over one million Black male voters was directly a result of the success of the Million Man March.

Today we are preparing for the Million Family March, to be convened on October 16, 2000, in Washington, D.C. The Million Family March will be broader and more expansive in terms of scope and outreach based on the standard set by the Million Man March.

The Million Family March, therefore, will involve mobilizing and organizing around the numerous public policy issues that impact the quality of life not only for Black Americans but also for Hispanic, Native, Asian and Pacific Islander, Arab and White Americans.

During the coming months we will support massive and ongoing voter-registration, education and turn-out-the-vote campaigns in every congressional district, state and region in the United States. The public policies outlined herein along with the analyses and programmatic plan of action will help us to achieve success on Monday October 16, 2000 in Washington, D.C. as well as the months and years that we will be engaging in follow-up action after The Million Family March.

We must continue to search for more effective means of communication and dissemination of information among our constituencies. We recognize that the social, political, economic and spiritual environment is dynamic and that constant reassessment will be a necessary element of any strategy.

THE NATIONAL AGENDA 2000-2008 of the Million Family March, is therefore the cumulative work-product of coalition-building, mutual clarification of issues, and commitment-bonding between Black, Hispanic, Native, Asian and Pacific Islander, Arab, and White Americans who seek to improve the quality of life of all families.

Reiterating The Million Man March and Day of Absence Mission Statement, we emphatically declare that we are "Conscious of the critical juncture of history in which we live and the challenges it poses for us."[3]

THE NATIONAL AGENDA 2000-2008 will not only be transmitted to the platform committees and leaders of the Democratic, Republican, and Reform Parties, but this agenda will also be reproduced and disseminated to millions of persons through a national network of newspapers, radio and television stations, Internet users, and grassroots newsletters. We intend to increase voter-registration, education, and mobilization in every state.

Our goal is to transform the political system by practicing the principle of coalition-building and by affirming a God-centered, spirit-filled, mass movement for social transformation and empowerment. May Allah (God) continue to bless our efforts with success.

Dr. Benjamin F. Muhammad
National Director, Million Family March

3. *Ibid.* p. 1.

A Vision for America

America is faced with the political and moral dilemma of reconciling pluralism and the inclusion of non-Whites with the democratic ideas espoused by the founding fathers. This is not a democracy in the fullest meaning of the word. Racism has to be overcome in order to gain a full expression of E Pluribus Unum (Out of the many, one). Is E Pluribus Unum meant to be interpreted as "Out of the many White ethnic strains, one people, or out of the many strains, White, Black and others, one people?"

Within the walls of this country there are two Americas, separate and unequal, White and Black (including other non-Whites). In order to reconcile these two Americas, the American people must come to terms with the limited vision of the founding fathers. The founding fathers didn't envision the current population profile, where the numbers of Black and Hispanic people are growing, threatening the majority status of Whites. Those who desire to maintain the old vision of White-rule under the name of democracy and pluralism will no longer be able to continue the subjugation of non-Whites. Now is the time for freedom, justice and equality for those who have been deprived of it.[4]

It is time, past time, for the entire human family to gain greater value in exchange for the vote. Black, Hispanic, Native, Asian and Pacific Islander, Arab and White Americans live in what would be the greatest democracy in the world. However, as the new millennium begins, there is dissatisfaction among Black, Hispanic, Native, Asian and Pacific Islander, Arab and White Americans in regard to equal and accountable representation in government.

Inequity, injustice, exclusion, and discrimination based on race, creed, and color, have prevented the United States of America from becoming a true democracy. Consequently, there are generations of those who have been alienated from participating in the political process. This non-participation only reinforces the absence of viable options for millions who desire and deserve a better quality of life.

The organization and mobilization for the Million Family March, to be convened on October 16, 2000, two weeks before the next national elections, offers an unprecedented opportunity to transform the social, political, economic, and spiritual landscape of America. We cannot afford to permit "business as usual," politically nor spiritually.

4.   Minister Louis Farrakhan, *A Torchlight For America*, FCN Publishing, 1993, Chicago, Illinois. p. 153.

THE NATIONAL AGENDA

Democracy is strengthened by full participation of the people in voter-registration and the casting of the vote. Maximizing the vote of the people is a powerful step towards social change and human progress.

We intend to inspire and motivate millions of families and communities to work together in the spirit of unity for freedom, justice, and equality for all.

FAMILY, MORALITY AND PUBLIC POLICY

FAMILY, MORALITY AND PUBLIC POLICY

The Root of America's Suffering

"Racism is the result of white supremacy as an ideology. Those poisoned by this ideology and philosophy can never give freedom, justice and equality or human rights to those who are non-White. In truth, they can never give true freedom, justice and equality even to those who are White. As a philosophy, white supremacy must die in order for the principles of freedom, justice and equality to live. The institutions under girded by this philosophy and the institutions poisoned by this philosophy must be purified in order that human beings can truly enjoy full human rights."[5]

The Honorable Minister Louis Farrakhan states:

America is clearly suffering, and from my vantage point, America lies on her deathbed in dire need of guidance and a new direction. If you examine her vital signs, you will have to agree that they show America is steadily on the decline.
The root of her suffering is basic immorality and vanity, where greed, lust and inordinate self-interest have become a way of life.
When the desire for the realization of self-interest becomes excessive, the first causality in this struggle is 'truth'.
The leaders in this society, in their struggle to achieve inordinate self-interest, engage in hiding the light of truth from the American people.[6]

Throughout the 20th Century, we witnessed the disintegration of the family unit as the basic pillar of society. The impact of world wars, industrialization, urbanization, and the sequential rise in structural alienation of family life have resulted in the devastation of millions of people and families.

The egalitarian principles embedded in the Constitution of the United States have not been equally applied to all the people who have labored and sacrificed in an attempt to make the American dream a reality. The nightmare of white supremacy and institutionalized racism, coupled with unfair economic policies, have prolonged poverty and social despair amidst the strongest sustained economic boom in the United States during the last fifty years.

5. *Statement from The Honorable Minister Louis Farrakhan, Convener of the Million Family March 2000, January 4, 2000.*
6. Minister Louis Farrakhan, *A Torchlight For America*, FCN Publishing, 1993, Chicago, Illinois, p. 1.

FAMILY, MORALITY AND PUBLIC POLICY

Black American families, Latino American families, Native American families, Asian and Pacific Islander American families, Arab American families, and White American families are suffering. The immorality of the tolerance of inequity and poverty is at the root of families suffering in America.

The moral imperative is to demand justice for all families and to challenge the systemic causes of the suffering of families and communities.

The following are some of the major issues in the national public policy debate concerning family and morality:

- Social welfare reform to ensure family stability
- Welfare to Workfare
- Family violence
- Early childhood pre-school preparation
- Early childhood development, support, and protection
- Support and protect grandparents and other family caregivers
- Support for single mothers with dependent children
- Immigration discrimination
- Social Security benefits
- Racism and economic inequity
- Language, ethnic, racial, and cultural discrimination
- Literacy and multi-lingual education
- Respect for Native American tribal rights concerning family
- Legislation supporting drug-free families and communities
- Equal access to continuing education for all family members

Immorality, vanity, greed, lust, avarice, deceit and failing to affirm the oneness of God and humanity all result in disobedience to the will of God which is the ultimate root of America's suffering. Blacks, Natives, Hispanics, Asian and Pacific Islanders, Arabs, and White Americans, as well as others all have suffered. Our families should atone, reconcile differences, and take responsibility to make the new millennium, the millennium of freedom, justice and equality for all.

Atonement:

A Prescription For Moral and Spiritual Renewal

If my people, which are called by my name, shall humble themselves and pray, and seek my face, and turn from their wicked ways; then will I hear from heaven, and will forgive their sin, and will heal their land.   —II Chronicles 7:14

The root of the problem in America is spiritual, necessitating a spiritual solution. (The president) should call for a convening of the spiritual leadership to spearhead a moral rejuvenation among the American people. Representatives of all races and all faiths should be brought to Washington, D.C., to hold conferences with (the president) and government leaders toward the aim of developing programs for building the values and moral backbone of America, and for building better race relations...

...A convening of the spiritual leadership with the leadership in government is a first step towards building the country's moral backbone. The central problems we should focus on are the basic value of human life, greed, criminal behavior and the treatment of women. It's the mistreatment of women that is the first act of criminal behavior in the society.[7]

Atonement is the seeking of forgiveness and guidance from Almighty God. The process of atonement includes the recognizing of the wrong, acknowledging the wrong, confessing to it, repenting from it, atoning for it, forgiving, reconciling and perfect union with Almighty God. Please note, however, that the process begins with recognition. Do we recognize the value of human life?

All life is created by God. The human family is blessed by the grace of God to strive for improvement and progress amidst a society and world gone mad with injustice and inequity. Disobedience to the righteous and just will of God has rendered our families vulnerable to exploitation and oppression.

Atonement is the prescription for moral and spiritual renewal. Black, Hispanic, Native, Asian and Pacific Islander, Arab, and White American families should engage in the eight steps of Atonement.

---

7.   Minister Louis Farrakhan, *A Torchlight For America*, FCN Publishing, 1993, Chicago, Illinois. p. 96-97.

Eight Steps of Atonement

1. Someone must point out the wrong
2. Acknowledgment of the wrong
3. Confess the fault; first to God, then to those offended
4. Repentance; a feeling of remorse or contrition or shame for the past conduct which was wrong and sinful
5. Atonement; meaning to make amends and reparations for the wrong
6. Forgiveness by the offended party; to cease to feel offense and resentment against another for the harm done
7. Reconciliation and restoration; meaning to become friendly and peaceable again
8. Perfect union with God

Atonement in the political sphere is also necessary. Too often public policies are legislated and codified without regard to the impact on the social condition of Black, Hispanic, Native, Asian and Pacific Islander, Arab and White Americans. Family life in America will be enhanced, as outlined above, through the eight steps of atonement. Morality in public policy serves the common good for all families and communities.

Declaration of Family Bill of Rights and Responsibility[8]

I. All families have the right to self-determination. Concurrently, all families have the responsibility to seek and secure moral and spiritual wellness of all of its members and the wellness and healing of the community in which they live.

II. All families have a right to a livable income to attain and maintain decent shelter, food, clothes, exposure to the arts and cultural integrity but also the responsibility to seek self-help, self-determination and shared responsibility for eliminating poverty and economic inequities.

III. All families have a right to live in safe, caring, drug free, and crime-free communities, but also the responsibility to foster public safety and sharing of resources.

IV. All families have a right to quality health care but also the responsibility to practice good health preserving habits such as proper diet, exercise and emotional well-being.

V. All families have the right to participate in the political process locally, nationally and globally. Concurrently, families have the duty to help govern themselves through informed voting, organizing, supporting and providing community-focused leadership in and outside of the family.

VI. All members of the family have a right to be free from physical and emotional abuse and also the responsibility to protect family members who are unable or ill prepared to protect themselves; assure governments that are sensitive and accountable to families and humanity.

VII. All families, irrespective of race, class or circumstance, have a right to live and work in unpolluted and environmentally safe communities, but also the responsibility to practice environmentally safe living habits and to respond to efforts to address environmental inequities in their communities; and to promote sustainable family and community development.

VIII. All families have a right to be free from inequities and discrimination based on immigration status, race, ethnicity, gender, age, and religion

8.   Rose Sanders, Esq., The Selma Alabama Voting Rights Museum, December 4, 1999.

FAMILY, MORALITY AND PUBLIC POLICY

but also the responsibility to internally and externally resist prejudice and bigotry.

IX. All families have a right for their children to be justly, truthfully and humanely educated, but also the responsibility to work for and demand these human essentials while supporting their children and the schools that serve them.

X. All families have a right to a just criminal and civil legal system, that restores and compensates the victims of unjust acts of laws and practices but also the responsibility to serve responsibly on juries, to demand that law makers are accountable to challenge or support those who challenge the death penalty, prosecutorial misconduct, inequities, unjust sentencing and inhumane prison conditions; and to seek restitution for families victimized by government sanctions and discrimination.

FAMILY, MORALITY AND PUBLIC POLICY

POLITICAL EMPOWERMENT

POLITICAL EMPOWERMENT

Political
Empowerment

Family is the basic unit of life in society. The political empowerment of our families requires more long-term involvement in the electoral process. To ensure political empowerment for all families in the United States, THE NATIONAL AGENDA 2000-2008 was drafted broad enough to be inclusive of the mutual political interests of Black, Hispanic, Native, Asian and Pacific Islander, Arab and White Americans.

In other words, through the Million Family March, a new viable national coalition of conscience and activism is in formation to achieve the goal of politically transforming American society through the significant increase of all families participating and challenging the existing political establishment. Progressive public policy should be legislated at local, state and federal levels.

"No business as usual in the political process" is the rallying cry of today. We focus on mobilizing the strongest possible progressive political force to leverage the advancement of the mutual interests of all who stand for the empowerment of our communities through the empowerment of our families.

Recommendations for action items
for political empowerment are as follows:

- Implement voter-education as vigorously as possible with the help of the Million Family March LOCs (Local Organizing Committees) and other local community organizations
- Convene local town hall meetings on THE NATIONAL AGENDA 2000-2008
- Hold state-wide meetings on THE NATIONAL AGENDA 2000-2008
- Establish direct solidarity with local communities and direct involvement in local politics and elections consistent with THE NATIONAL AGENDA 2000-2008 and local agendas determined by LOCs and other local organizations
- Citizenship-education programs and seminars

- Youth voter-registration and political education in high schools
- Grassroots organizing and political platform mobilizing through door-to-door campaigns
- Challenge unjust voter-registration practices in localities
- Improve ballot access laws and equal access to media
- Support campaign finance reform
- Proportional representation
- Advocate the right to unrestricted spiritual and cultural expression, and organize community voter-education on behalf of our houses of worship
- Link the political agenda of Black, Hispanic, Native, Asian and Pacific Islander, Arab and White Americans with the political agenda of the Third World and the poor and oppressed worldwide
- Work to extend and expand the Voting Rights Act
- Advocate for the creation and maintenance of voting redistricting that provides more representation and equitable government
- Restoration of voting rights for persons after completing time served in prison
- Conduct national polls and research to promote a more effective engagement of the political process

POLITICAL EMPOWERMENT

Voting Rights

Ensure Equal Access To Full Voter Participation[9]

For the first time in almost 30 years, minorities are actually losing, rather than gaining, full voter-participation. Given a green light by the Supreme Court, federal courts and state legislatures are seeking to dismantle majority-minority districts.

Background

The 15th and 19th Amendments to the Constitution guarantee African Americans (men and women) the right to vote. For many decades, however, discrimination prevented African Americans from voting. To remedy this, Congress passed the Voting Rights Act of 1965. As amended, the Act permanently bars voting discrimination and provides special enforcement mechanisms that will expire in 2007, if not re-authorized by Congress. Even if the enforcement mechanisms end, African Americans' constitutionally-guaranteed right to vote will not expire.

The Million Family March supports the continued enforcement of the Voting Rights Act, the National Voting Rights Act and the National Voter Registration Act as partial remedies for the systemic political disenfranchisement of communities and families.

Today, because of the Act, there are over 8,000 African American elected officials nationwide, with 5,000 of them elected from the South. There are 39 African American members of the CBC, including over one-third elected from the South. Most of these officials were elected from majority-minority districts.

However, just as minorities have begun electing representatives of their choice, their full voter-participation is threatened. In a series of cases, including *Shaw v. Reno* and, *Miller v. Johnson*, the Supreme Court and other lower courts have declared several majority-minority districts unconstitutional.

The National Asian Pacific American Consortium, (NAPAC) and its affiliates; The Asian Pacific American Legal Center, The Asian American Legal Defense and Educational Fund, and The Asian Law Caucus, "con-

9. Congressional Black Caucus, *The Agenda: 1997-1999*, 105th Congress of the United States, Washington, D.C., p. 18.

POLITICAL EMPOWERMENT

ducted exit poll surveys in the 1994, 1996 and 1998 general elections and monitored compliance with the bilingual assistance provisions of the Voting Rights Act in their region. The surveys document the need for bilingual assistance in removing barriers to voting."[10]

Goals[11]

- Ensure enforcement of all laws which protect and encourage the right to vote for all citizens
- Defend the creation of districts that provide opportunities for all citizens to be represented by candidates of their choice
- Consider alternative solutions to maintain and expand minority representation in elective bodies

10.   NAPAC, Internet: www.napalc.org/content/pro_voting.html.
11.   *Ibid.*

POLITICAL EMPOWERMENT

Census 2000

The 1990 Census resulted in 26 million errors, an undercount of 8.4 million people and 3% of U.S. children not being counted. In addition, while the national undercount average was 1.6%, the undercount of Latino Americans was more than three times this average, or 5 percent. Other minority groups were also undercounted, for example Native Americans 4.5% and African Americans 4.4 percent. As a direct result of this undercount, many individuals were effectively denied government representation.[12]

The Congressional Hispanic Caucus (CHC) supports the use of proven and reliable scientific methods to complement the Census bureau's aggressive enumeration effort. The Census bureau's plan will utilize both the traditional head count method and scientific statistical methods to arrive at the most accurate count possible. Using modern methods will result in a national undercount of less than .01 percent. A vast improvement from the 5% Latino American undercount of 1990.

- CHC will work with the Census bureau at the grassroots level to inform and educate Latino Americans across the country about the upcoming census. Grassroots campaigns will be undertaken to motivate community members to participate in the 2000 Census.
  - A national plan targeting high Latino American undercount areas needs to be undertaken.
  - Through its membership, the CHC will expand the lines of communication with national, regional and local organizations to work in a comprehensive plan that minimizes the Latino American undercount.
- Asian and Pacific Islanders were undercounted in the 1990 Census by 2.3% or 160,000 individuals.[13]

The undercount in the Census of any community or racial group in the United States will undermine the potential of that community or racial group to increase political empowerment. In addition, an undercount by the Census bureau will prevent communities from getting the accurate proportional federal funding for public education, crime prevention, health care

12. Congressional Hispanic Caucus, *Legislative Priorities: 1999*, 106th Congress of the United States, Washington, D.C., p. 7.
13. The National Asian Pacific American Legal Consortium, Internet: naplc.org/content/pro_Census1_2.html. Lessons from the 1990 Census: The Undercount and the Asian Pacific American Community.

POLITICAL EMPOWERMENT

and transportation. Also, undercounted communities will not get their fair share of proportional representation in Congress, states legislatures and local governments. Civil rights that prohibits discrimination against minorities in undercounted communities in education, voting, housing and employment will not be adequately enforced.[14]

According to the Congressional Black Caucus, "The U.S. Census Bureau has missed millions of persons conducting each decennial Census, especially minorities, the poor, children, newly arrived immigrants, and the homeless." The CBC further stated, "An accurate Census is vital to every community." Last year, Census data was used in the distribution of more than $180 billion in federal aid. "Accurate Census data is the only way to assure that local communities receive their 'fair share' of federal spending; an inaccurate count will shortchange the affected communities for an entire decade."[16]

POLITICAL EMPOWERMENT

14. *Ibid.*
15. CBC News, Vol. 1, No. 1, April 1999, p. 13: *"Census 2000: Ensuring a Fair and Accurate Count of Every Person."*
16. *Ibid.*

Coalition Priorities

Coalition-building among families across the lines of race, religion and culture is a necessity to give birth to a new paradigm for socioeconomic and political transformation. Therefore, towards the goal of progressive change, it is in the best interest to work in coalition with others who share common oppression, common issues, and common visions. We are compelled by an understanding of God's law to include to the greatest extent possible, all the masses. The purpose is to assure that justice and equity are the products of our every action. All individuals, organizations, and entities must have their needs, interests, health and rights protected to the extent that they can work towards a harmonious society. We cannot work as a disconnected whole. We can only be whole when we have attained a God-consciousness and have affirmed the unity of the entire human family.

Recognizing our cultural, ethnic, religious and other differences, our mission maintains that coalition policies must be implemented to address the collective whole. To this end we shall draw upon the best concepts and ideas that each group has to offer. This outreach shall take place on a family by family and a community by community basis as well as on a national basis.

While there exists a multitude of constituent groups throughout this nation, their interests can be composed into principled dialogue which results in common policies which may be used by all. Although we have differences, we also have similarities. Our commonalties are what we shall draw upon and build upon. Coalition-building is one of the mechanisms by which the key issues of this forum shall be disseminated throughout the world. All issues raised shall have a particular definition, reason and purpose. We shall utilize our natural affection, compassion and creative good will to implement a holistic policy for each key issue.

Black Americans, Native Americans, Hispanic Americans, Asian and Pacific Islander Americans and Arab Americans have historically had to live with the same oppressive conditions as other oppressed people throughout the world. The violations against these and other ethnic and religious groups have been perpetuated by white supremacy using the same tools and methodologies. Some of the interests of Native Americans are the violations of treaty agreements and sovereignty rights, and the respect for the sacredness of Native lands. The concerted effort to bring their population to total extinction is barbaric and genocidal.

The Latin American community has been treated with undisputed indignity regarding immigration and unfair labor and trade practices. Asian Americans have also been victimized by racial hatred in terms of racial stereotypes. In recent years, Arab Americans have become the target of racial intolerance and are increasingly viewed as scapegoats. Now recogniz-

POLITICAL EMPOWERMENT

ing these facts we have a context with which to work towards a common struggle and a common victory.

POLITICAL EMPOWERMENT

Civil Rights

Protect and Renew Enforcement[17]

Discrimination is a reality in America. While minorities have made gains over the past 30 years, America has not become a color-blind society.

Background

In recent years, several high-profile discrimination cases–Texaco, Circuit City, Pitney Bowes and Denny's, to name a few–have resulted in huge settlements or judgments against large corporations. African American employees have sued these corporations for discrimination in hiring, transfers and promotions.

These cases illustrate how pervasive and embedded discrimination still is in America. In fact, discrimination claims have risen by almost 115 percent over the past few years.

There currently is a backlog of over 77,000 cases filed with the Equal Employment Opportunity Commission (EEOC), the government agency responsible for investigating and enforcing workplace discrimination.

Goals[18]

- Increase funding for the EEOC and overall federal enforcement of civil rights laws
- Eliminate the backlog of discrimination complaints pending at the EEOC
- Create a dialogue with key corporations to facilitate diversity and open the doors to opportunities for all Americans

POLITICAL EMPOWERMENT

---

17. Congressional Black Caucus, *The Agenda: 1997-1999*, 105th Congress of the United States, Washington, D.C., p. 19.
18. *Ibid.*

SECTION 3

JUSTICE ISSUES

Law and Justice

*The principle of justice is the second greatest principle that constitutes the meaning of life. Without justice there is no joy in being free so, we can say that justice is the joy of freedom. Justice is represented in the universe by the stars and without justice there is no balance in the human mind. The more injustice that we suffer, the more imbalance is the result on the human mind. From the imbalance of the mind comes actions that are considered anti-social and criminal but the cause goes back to the principle of justice. ustice is fair-dealing. Justice is that which distinguishes right from wrong. Justice is the weapon that God will use in the Day of Judgment. Justice is a human need therefore justice is a human right. The principle of fair-dealing and equity starts in the home with parents who are balanced and practice fairness in dealing with each other and their children. If love is the foundation out of which we act then we would act equitably and fairly with one another. Justice is righteousness and it is only justice or righteousness that promotes love and strengthens the bond between human beings. The greatest principle of justice was spoken by Jesus and it is called **The Golden Rule. Do unto others as you would have others do unto you.***

*Prophet Muhammad (Peace and Blessings be Upon Him) restated this Golden Rule in this manner: **We have not attained to righteousness or justice until we love for our brother what we love for ourselves.***

All the nations of the earth claim to believe in egalitarian principles, or principles of equality and fairness. There are no two things in the universe that are alike. Therefore, things in creation are not equal in size, shape, density, talent, beauty, but that which renders all things equal is the law under which all things are created. No matter whether we are rich or poor, White or Black, noble or ignoble, wise or foolish, the only way we can come onto this planet is by the law of birth.

So, birth renders us all equal and those who come on to the planet at some time have to leave and death is a law that renders us all equal. It is only that which is between these two great laws, birth and death, the law of life, that is administered by human beings who are less than what we should be so that inequity abounds and wherever there is inequity there is injustice. In the word equality is another word - qualification. We must qualify ourselves in order to be considered equal. Therefore, opportunity denied disallows the human being to qualify himself or herself for equality and it denies the human being the principle of justification of his or her existence. So, equality of opportunity is a basic human need therefore equality of opportunity is a human right. [19]

19.   *Statement from The Honorable Minister Louis Farrakhan, Convener of the Million Family March 2000, January 4, 2000.*

JUSTICE ISSUES

Racial Profiling

Racism is a disease. It spreads like a contagious lethal virus of white supremacy. Racial profiling is an insidious form of racial discrimination and the denial of fundamental human rights. All people are ultimately impacted, yet the cold damp hand of oppression continues to be placed more harshly on the shoulders of people of color in America.

The Joint Center for Political and Economic Studies, based in Washington, D.C., issued a policy alert entitled, "The Perils of Driving While Black: Civil Rights Organizations are Suing Law Enforcement Agencies That Stop Black and Latino Motorist Because They Fit a Racial Profile."[20]   The alert stated, "News accounts of police profiling are becoming more and more common. These documents are exposing a widespread assault on the civil liberties of people of color throughout society."[21]

Air travelers who have a "middle eastern" appearance are frequently profiled racially and stopped unjustly by law enforcement personnel.[22]

Racial profiling is broadly defined in the United States to encompass any actions taken by a law enforcement officer during an automobile traffic stop, or at an airport prior to or after travel, that is based upon racial or ethnic stereotypes, and that has the affect of treating minority travelers differently that non-minority travelers which is in violation of both the civil and human rights of minority travelers.[23]

According to the New Jersey Attorney General, the problem of racial profiling is not a new problem; it is a problem that has persisted for a long period of time. "Although the racial profiling issue has recently gained state and national attention, the underlying conditions that foster disparate treatment of minorities have existed for decades in New Jersey and throughout the nation and will not be changed overnight"[24]

Racial Profiling is a National Problem

The scope of the problem of racial profiling is evident in the series of remedial legislation that is now being proposed in several states including, Florida, North Carolina, Maryland, Virginia, Rhode Island, Massachusetts,

---

20. David C. Ruffin, FOCUS, Joint Center for Political and Economic Studies, Vol. 27, No. 3; Washington, D.C., March 1999, p. 3.
21. *Ibid.*
22. *Ibid.*
23. Peter Verniero and Paul H. Zoubek, Office of New Jersey Attorney General, *"Interim Report of the State Police Review Team Regarding Allegations of Racial Profiling"*, April 20, 1999, Trenton, N.J. p. 5.
24. *Ibid*, p. 3.

Arkansas, Illinois and California.[25]

Most of the state legislation being introduced is similar to a bill originally drafted by Congressman John Conyers of Michigan, the "Traffic Stops: Statistics Acts of 1997."[26] The Bill before Congress today is known as HR 1443, the Traffic Stops Statistics Act of 1999.[27]

One of the more explicit and detailed accounts and analysis of the magnitude of the problem of racial profiling was published by the American Civil Liberties Union (ACLU).[28] In a June 1999 special report entitled, "Driving While Black: Racial Profiling on Our Nation's Highways," the ACLU emphasized, "Police abuse against people of color is a legacy of African American enslavement, repression and legal inequality"[29]

Under the pretense of carrying out a "war on drugs," persons have been targeted for harassment not based on involvement with drugs but based on race and creed. The ACLU reported:

> *Significant blame for this rampant abuse of power also can be laid at the feet of the government's misguided crusade enthusiastically enforced by lawmakers and administrations of both parties at every level of government. From the outset, the war on drugs has in fact been a war on people and their constitutional rights, with African Americans, Latino Americans and other minorities bearing the brunt of the damage. It is a war that has, among other depredations, spawned racist profiles and supposed drug couriers on our nation's highways. Today, police ostensibly looking for drug criminals routinely stop drivers based on the color of their skin. This practice is so common that the minority community has given it the divisive term, "Driving while Black or Brown."[30]*

Constitutionally, the Fourth Amendment prohibits this type of intrusion by the police in acts not justified by the law. "But recent Supreme Court decisions allow police to use traffic stops as a pretext to 'fish' for evidence. Both anecdotal and quantitative data show that nationwide, the police exercise this discretionary power primarily against African Americans and Latinos."[31]

Research has also exposed that racial profiling is not limited exclusively to police misconduct. At airports Arabs and others are routinely subjected to searches and unjustified harassment. Even inside the United States Department of Energy and other government agencies and departments,

25. *Ibid,* p. 60.
26. *Ibid.*
27. *Ibid,* p. 61.
28. American Civil Liberties Union, Internet: www.aclu.org/profiling/report/index.html.
29. *Ibid.*
30. *Ibid.*
31. *Ibid.*

there is evidence of the existence of racial profiling in employment discrimination. On January 19, 2000, the U.S. Secretary of Energy, Bill Richardson, released an agency task force report on racial profiling within the Department of Energy. Richardson stated, "I formed this task force because I was concerned that Asian Pacific Americans at our labs were feeling their patriotism and loyalty were questioned in the wake of allegations about Chinese espionage. As a Hispanic, I know first-hand the damage of racial stereotyping."[32]

Action Items

- Propose and enact legislation to end the use of pretext stops by law enforcement officials on highways
- Support the Traffic Stops Statistics Study Act
- Minotor racial profiling statewide, state by state
- Encourage U.S. Justice Department to take steps to end racial profiling in federally funded programs
- Require periodic racial sensitivity training for state and local highway police officers
- End racial profiling in airports,train stations, bus terminals and all other transportation ports

32. United States United States Department of Energy,
     Internet: home.doe.gov/news/release00/janpr/pr00011.htm.

Police Brutality

The Million Family March opposes police brutality. In response to the significant increase in acts of racially-motivated police brutality, abuse and misconduct in the major cities across the United States, the Congressional Black Caucus sponsored unprecendeted hearings in Washington, D.C., New York, Chicago and Los Angeles in 1999. During the hearing on police brutality in Washington, D.C., the Washington office of the American Civil Liberties Union testified, "The federal government has been quite willing to fund programs designed to get officers on the street. It has been considerably less willing to ensure that the officers' conduct is appropriate once they are on the street."[33]

It has been difficult to bring police officers to trial for their crimes of police brutality. Even in highly publicized cases such as those of Abner Louima, Tyisha Miller and Amadou Diallo, police officers have been exposed in cover-ups, obstruction of justice and conspiracy to prevent the truth from being made public.

New York City Police Officers, Thomas Wiese, Thomas Bruder and Charles Schwarz face five-year sentences on charges of conspiracy and obstruction of justice for lying in an attempt to protect officer Schwarz, who was convicted in the summer of 1999 for holding down Abner Louima inside of the bathroom of the 70th police precinct while Police Officer Justin Volpe sexually attacked Louima, a Haitian American immigrant.

Once again, in New York City as well as Los Angeles and all large cities, the issue of police brutality demands a public policy response.

The trial of the police officers responsible for firing 41 gun shots at unarmed West African immigrant, Amadou Diallo, hitting him 19 times, is another tragic reminder of the lethal impact of police brutality. The National Urban League issued the following statement:

> *Amadou Diallo lived in the Bronx. He died in the Bronx. He deserves to have justice in the Bronx. {Instead, the trail will be moved to the state capital in Albany, 150 miles away.}*
> *But, justice for Amadou Diallo will not come in the Bronx, because a New York State appeals court panel ruled that the ensuing publicity about the shooting and the demonstrations it provoked have made it impossible for the police officers to get a fair trial. This decision is a blow to the trust in the criminal justice system people from all sides of the color line have been laboring to build.*[34]

33. Congressional Black Caucus News, Vol. 1, No. 2, August 1999.
34. Hugh B. Price, National Urban League, "*To Be Equal*," New York, N.Y., January 2000.

Juvenile Justice

Provide Alternatives for Our Youth[35]

No one is born a criminal. Proposals that seek to punish but not prevent juvenile crime cannot succeed in the long run.

Background

Studies show that the number of youth will increase dramatically over the next few decades. Despite an actual decrease in juvenile crime, many conservatives are urging radical new policies in response to this rise. These new "get tough" proposals include imposing mandatory minimum sentences, trying youths as adults, locking them up with adult offenders, and eliminating many prevention programs. However, these "get tough" solutions do not work. Instead, prevention strategies such as community policing account for the recent decline in juvenile crime.

In addition, "get tough" efforts, particularly those dealing with drugs, have a disproportionate impact on minority youth. Until 1981, the drug arrest rate for White youth was higher than that for African American youth. By 1992, however, African American juveniles in California, for example, were seven times more likely than White juveniles to be jailed for similar serious drug offenses. African American youth were also referred to juvenile court at a rate twice that of their White counterparts.

Goals

- Increase resources for crime prevention and youth activities to reduce the likelihood of juvenile crime
- Fight efforts to impose mandatory minimum sentences for juvenile offenders
- Oppose efforts to incarcerate our youth with adult offenders
- Support community-based organizations, including the Boys and Girls Clubs, and other programs that prevent juvenile crime
- Propose legislative initiatives to increase education and opportunities for at-risk youth

35. Congressional Black Caucus, *The Agenda: 1997-1999*, 105th Congress of the United States, Washington, D.C., p. 24.

JUSTICE ISSUES

The human brain produces certain hormones and chemicals that give pleasure, help us bear pain, and help us to survive grief and the loss of loved ones.

God knew that He created life with the purpose of struggle and it is only through struggle that we attain to the greatness of character that causes us to be a reflection of God. So, in the struggle of life there are disappointments and there are chemicals in the brain that can help us bear the pain of disappointment.

Since God created life and is the ultimate cause of death, knowing that each of us at some point in life will lose a friend, a family member, a teacher to death, God has created within us that which would give us the ability to bear the pain of their losses and go on with our lives.

Since we are living in a very unusual time period, a time period unlike any period in the history of man and his struggle, there is a greater demand on our brains to produce what we need for balance in a time of extraordinary loss. By the time! Surely man is in loss.

Associated with loss is grief and when you live in the time of judgment when the weapon that God uses is justice – that as a man soweth the same shall he also reap, then this is a time of extraordinary pull on the natural hormonal secretion of the brain.

In a time when the consequences of our actions are coming back quickly against us, there is a depletion of the body's natural response to the natural vicissitudes of life. As a result, the chemists are making billions and billions of dollars creating drugs that give the human being what the brain, under normal circumstances, was able to give. There is so much sadness in the world because we live in a time of war and revolution, pestilence, famine, earthquakes and natural disasters. Drugs have been introduced into the society to take the place of God, the peace that belief in God can give and the strength that faith in God can give to allow every human being to handle the most difficult situations in their lives. It is the lack of faith in God, the lack of trust in God, that allows us to put our trust in things. So, man's trust is in drugs, man's trust is in guns, man's trust is in the things that cannot really give peace, as a result, suicide, AIDS, and all manner of disease and destructive behavior is now plaguing human beings.

Our lifestyle is based on ignorance of life, as a result the scripture is true, **There is a way that seemeth right unto a man, but, the ends thereof are the ways of death**.

Once the human being is reconnected to God, the Source of strength and power, the Source of knowledge, the Source of healing, then connection to that Source allows the human being to believe that there is no burden too great for him or her to bear and there is no impediment too large or too strong that, with faith, he or she *cannot remove.*[36]

Drugs: Free Our Families and Communities from Drugs[37]

The human destruction from drugs has become so commonplace that in some communities many have lost hope.

Background

The federal government currently spends $15 billion dollars each year on law enforcement, treatment and prevention programs in its so-called "war on drugs." Despite these programs, the human costs of drugs are staggering:

- According to the Black Community Crusade for Children, each day in America -- 94 African American children are arrested for drug offenses, 151 are arrested for crimes of violence, and 1,118 are victims of violent crimes.
- While African American men comprise 6% of the total population, they represent 35% of drug arrests, 55% of drug convictions and 74% of those serving prison sentences for drug-related offenses.
- Almost 40 percent of those infected with HIV/AIDS are intravenous drug abusers.

Goals[38]

- Increase funding for drug prevention, treatment and education for at-risk communities
- Refocus federal resources to target and punish large-scale drug smugglers, suppliers and distributors
- Propose enhanced sentences for law enforcement personnel convicted of drug-related offenses
- Establish faith-centered treatment programs
- Organize town hall meetings, workshops and educational forums to take our drug eradication message to communities across the nation
- Eliminate sentencing disparities
- Investigate allegations of involvement in drug trafficking by intelligence agencies

36. *Statement from The Honorable Minister Louis Farrakhan, Convener of the Million Family March 2000, January 4, 2000.*
37. Congressional Black Caucus, *The Agenda: 1997-1999*, 105th Congress of the United States, Washington, D.C., p. 3.
38. *Ibid.*

Drug Sentencing: Eliminate Disparities[39]

While we must find solutions to the crack cocaine epidemic destroying our communities, the inherent unfairness in the sentencing disparities for crack and powdered cocaine offenses cannot be justified.

Background

According to the Office of National Drug Control Policy, young Whites, ages 18-25, use crack cocaine at a higher percentage (3.2%) than young African Americans (1.8%). However, the penalties and prosecutions for crack cocaine cases are disproportionately applied to minorities.

While the decision to change crack and powdered cocaine offenses in either federal or state court is typically discretionary, federal convictions for cocaine offenses carry mandatory minimum sentences. Minorities currently account for 96 percent of federal crack cocaine prosecutions and convictions.

Under federal law, the ratio of powdered cocaine to crack cocaine is 100-to-1. This means that for sentencing purposes, 500 grams of powdered cocaine is the equivalent of five grams of crack cocaine. For example, a White defendant selling 500 grams of powdered cocaine is likely to get one year in the federal system, while an African American defendant selling five grams of crack cocaine likely will be prosecuted in federal court, and if convicted, will receive a mandatory minimum sentence of five years.

African Americans are now incarcerated at a rate nearly eight times to that of Whites. The July 1997 proposal by President Clinton to reduce the ratio to 10-to-1 did not eliminate this unfairness.

Moreover, recent charges that in the mid-1980s, the Central Intelligence Agency (CIA), Nicaraguan Contras and others trafficked in drugs have heightened concerns about unfairness and raised questions about the connection between U.S. foreign policy and drugs.

Goals

- Equalize disparate sentencing guidelines for crack and powdered cocaine
- Develop legislation to eliminate selective prosecution of minorities in drug-related offenses
- Seek investigations of alleged links between American foreign policy and international drug smuggling operation

---

39. Congressional Black Caucus, *The Agenda: 1997-1999*, 105th Congress of the United States, Washington, D.C., p. 21.

JUSTICE ISSUES

Drugs: The Family And The United States Government

News articles published in *The Final Call News*[40] cited evidence linking the U.S. Central Intelligence Agency to the introduction of crack cocaine into Black and Latino communities, with the drug profits used to fund the CIA-backed operations such as the support of the Nicaraguan Contra army in the early 1980s.

These disclosures, which are based on a series of reports originating from the San Jose Mercury News, verify long-held suspicions of the U.S. government's programmatic involvement in destroying and undermining growth and development within the Black community.

The history of the U.S. government's involvement in this type of hostile activity against the African American community is long and continuous. As such, it is important for African Americans to understand their need to work vigorously to eliminate and eradicate drug use and drug sales as an option in our communities. Drug use and sales must be viewed as an act of treason and this activity must be looked at as it is: ***A threat to the very survival of every man, woman and child in the community.***

Furthermore, we must use the criminal laws to prosecute all government officials involved in the drug trade.

We recognize that the criminal justice system is unjust. We further affirm, however, that families should live in a crime-free environment.

Law, Justice, And Prisons Action Items

- Establish a community court system and community custody where non-violent offenders remain in the custody of houses of worship and community organizations
- Allocate more funds to education instead of prisons
- Closely monitor all arrests and all law enforcement activities
- Establish civilian complaint review boards
- Establish Manhood training and self-protection form incarceration centers
- Abolition of the death penalty
- Abolition of "three strikes and you're out" legislation
- Prevent passage of "one strike" legislation in public housing arrests
- Lobby for a moratorium on prison construction
- Force the abolition of mandatory minimum sentences
- Force the abolition of sentencing disparities, such as the one between crack and powdered cocaine, for poor and oppressed communities
- Strategies for more judicial appointments reflective of the demo-

40.   *The Final Call News*, FCN Publishing, Chicago, Illinois, Volume 15, No. 32 – 33.

graphic profile of society and the community

- Demand that the racial and gender composition of the Supreme Court be truly representative of the demography of American society
- Legislation to ensure the prevention of police misconduct and brutality
- Prevent disproportionate application of mandatory sentencing
- Abolition of racial profiling in law enforcement
- Challenge the racist use of "zero tolerance" policies by both law enforcement and school system officials

JUSTICE ISSUES

FAMILY, MORALITY AND PUBLIC POLICY

Prison Reform

Since we live in a world that is contrary to that which is of God, a world of injustice and a world of unrighteousness, the consequence of that is the behavior of human beings that causes the human to act as a savage. A savage is a human being that has lost the knowledge of self and is living the life of a beast.

When we have a society filled with persons that prey on one another, then we have a society of people that are living on an animalistic plane of existence and therefore prisons are built to house those who offend the laws of men who have already offended the laws of God. These prisons have proved that they do not have the will, the desire or knowledge of how to reform the inmates. As a result, there is a very high rate of recidivism. True prison reform can only come by giving the human being those human rights that were deprived by society and by the ignorance of parents and the family.

When white supremacy, rules of the society, and the society becomes fearful of the population growth of the Black American and the Latino American, then society increases the means by which anti-social behavior will become more prevalent and therefore the building of prisons is the biggest growth industry in America. People do not build hotels because they do not expect occupancy. Businessmen invest in prisons that they do not intend to fill. True prison reform starts with the enlightenment of the inmate of who that inmate is in reality and not what he or she has become because of circumstances. True prison reform reconnects the soul to its Creator and begins to provide those human needs and then we see a change in attitude in the inmate that leads to behavioral change.[41]

The disproportionate incarceration of Black Americans, Hispanic Americans, Native Americans and others in the United States is a crisis of mammoth proportions that we must address. In many places, up to 50 percent of persons from our communities are on probation, parole or in jail. Our failure to address this crisis will greatly diminish our family power and voting power.

Too often we allow our incarcerated sisters and brothers to be forgotten and disconnected from the community. As we work to raise the cultural and political consciousness of our families in public housing and ghettos, and in the suburbs and upscale areas, we must also work to raise the cultural and political consciousness of our family members in the jail cells and chain gangs, and in the soli-

---

41 *Statement from The Honorable Minister Louis Farrakhan, Convener of the Million Family March 2000, January 4, 2000.*

tary wings and death rows. It is the responsibility of those of us on the "outside" to provide the imprisoned with information, support and encouragement both while they are behind bars and as they re-enter society.

Federal, state, and local governments consign many of us to a life of prison numbers, overcrowded cells, parole hearings and disenfranchisement by planning to imprison us rather than planning to educate us. Many of our sisters and brothers have their dreams and aspirations killed by a society which enacts and legitimizes racially discriminatory laws and encourages and justifies the disproportionately high brutalization, harassment, and scrutinizing of our communities by police.

To the contrary, we must work to provide all people with a life of academic opportunity, spiritual growth, family development, and community support. We must win the hearts and minds of our people and inspire them to dream and produce an environment which nurtures their dreams and transforms them into reality. When others have given up on our people, we must invest in our people. When others push our people to despair, we must push them to hope. When others declare that our people are irredeemable, we must believe that they are redeemable, and convince them of that as well.

Goals

- Provide incarcerated persons with an avenue for community participation and support
- Raise the cultural and political consciousness of the incarcerated
- Prevent incarcerated inmates from being abused or lost in the system, as a result of their own actions or as a result of government neglect or misconduct
- To this end, the Prison Outreach Initiative seeks to match incarcerated persons with people on the "outside" who will:
  ° Visit the incarcerated sister or brother regularly
  ° Send correspondence to the incarcerated sister or brother regularly
  ° Provide the incarcerated sister or brother with reading materials
  ° Raise small amounts of money for the incarcerated sister's or brother's canteen account
- Monitor the general treatment and parole status of those incarcerated from our communities
- Help persons returning from prison
- Establish community-based halfway houses and other alternatives to institutionalization
- Funds to evaluate faith-house programs

Political Prisoners

We have political prisoners and prisoners of war incarcerated in prisons and jails all across America. We have Mumia Abu Jamal unjustly on death row in Pennsylvania. Geronimo Pratt is now free, but still faces a retrial, even though the government knows that he is innocent of the crime for which he was convicted. Leonard Peltier, a Native American political prisoner, continues to be held unjustly for over 25 years. Assata Shakur remains exiled in Cuba after escaping the brutal political imprisonment imposed on her unjustly by the State of New Jersey during the 1970's. The stories of COINTELPRO's involvement in the manufacturing, doctoring, concealing and manipulation of evidence to make sure that revolutionaries are kept off the streets and behind bars are legendary, yet the majority of the leadership turn a blind eye to the reality of the existence of political prisoners and prisoners of war in this country.

What is the Problem?

The list of political prisoners is long and their sentences are even longer. The government of the United States would have you believe that these people are common criminals. The United States government waged an orchestrated campaign to demonize, vilify and criminalize these people in the eyes of the community and the world prior to bringing them to trial and during the years of their incarceration. On a broad scale they've done their job well–so well in fact that even the most progressive elements of our community hesitate to even speak about the existence of political prisoners when they come together and when you bring it up, they change the conversation. We are asking that:

- Community leaders pick up the mantle with us and make the call strong and loud for the continuation of the hearings into COIN-TELPRO and its role in the imprisonment of political prisoners and prisoners of war.
- Increase community awareness on the issue of the existence of political prisoners.
- Organize forums and speaking engagements in local areas through Million Family March Local Organizing Committees so that we can more effectively make known to our community that there are people in prison who have been there for years and who were/are willing to sacrifice their lives to make a better world for all of us.

JUSTICE ISSUES

- Write political prisoners and let them know you care and encourage others to do the same and establish local writing clubs and other mechanisms to communicate with political prisoners.

Relief for Central Americans – Parity for Salvadorians, Guatemalans and Hondurans.

The Congressional Hispanic Caucus is opposed to singling out one group of immigrants for favorable treatment. The Nicaraguan Adjustment and Central American Relief Act (NACARA) left approximately 250,000 Salvadorians and Guatemalans with an unresolved immigration status.

- NACARA regulations and the "Extreme hardship" determination for Salvadorians and Guatemalans: The administration has an opportunity to make a group-based determination of hardship for these deserving immigrants, allowing them to stay and continue contributing to the battered economies of their home countries.
- The CHC will support legislation HR36 which provides nationals from El Salvador, Guatemala, Honduras and Haiti the opportunity to apply for adjustment of status under NACARA. The administration should make this a legislative priority in the 106th Congress.

Late Amnesty - Section 377

A legislative or administrative solution should be found for the thousands of immigrants who have been in the United States on or before January 1, 1982. As a result of Section 377, thousands of hard-working, tax-paying individuals have begun to lose their work permits and have been forced to go underground and will face the imminent danger of deportation.
- "Late amnesty" individuals should be reissued working permits while a solution to their cases is finalized.
- The pending applications for "late amnesty" individuals who have been found eligible should be promptly processed by the Immigration and Naturalization Service (INS).
- A legislative solution for the individuals that are not covered by the administrative measures should be found.

---

42. Congressional Hispanic Caucus, *Legislative Priorities: 1999*, 106th Congress of the United States, Washington, D.C., p. 5.

JUSTICE ISSUES

Naturalization Backlog

- There are currently over 1.7 million individuals that are waiting to become U.S. citizens. The CHC will monitor the INS's progress in the processing of naturalization applications to ensure that applications are processed expeditiously and fairly.
- The processing of naturalization applications must not only be efficient but also fair. The CHC is concerned about the increasing number of naturalization applications being denied. For instance, in the Los Angeles office, in the first quarter of FY1999, 43 percent of the "completed applications" were denied – that is about 38,000 of the 68,000 applications processed in the Los Angeles area.

Adjustment of status 245(I)

Section 245(I) allowed immigrants eligible under the existing quota system who had "fallen out of status" to apply for permanent residence in the United States. Section 245(I) expired in November 1997 and now immigrants must return to their home country to apply for permanent residence. Without Section 245(I), people eligible to become green card holders can be barred from returning to the U.S. for a period of three to ten years. Section 245(I) should be restored.

Restoration of Benefits for Legal Immigrants

(Please refer to the Health Task Force priorities)

H-2A Guest worker/Bracero program

The administration and members of Congress should not support any proposal that would expand this program. The General Accounting Office (GAO) reported in December 1997 that no farm-worker labor shortages exist, therefore, there is no justification for the administration and members of Congress to support such an initiative. To import foreign agricultural workers would pose a threat to American jobs and undermine the protection of agricultural workers' basic needs.

Public Charge

(Please refer to the Health Task Force priorities)

INS Restructuring

- Monitor the restructuring process to ensure that the enforcement and service components are developed in a balanced manner.

INS Enforcement Strategy

- Ensure that in its enforcement undertakings, the INS does not violate the civil liberties of any individual.

Secret Evidence

Arab Americans and other minorities are increasingly alarmed about the unconstitutional use of secret evidence by the Immigration and Naturalization Service (INS).[43] The use of secret evidence by the INS in legal proceedings against Arab Muslims immigrants is a justice issue deserving greater public awareness and involvement.

"In 2000, the Arab American political and electoral agenda is aimed at protecting our civil and constitutional rights and ensuring that the promise of freedom and equality applies to all Americans."[44] The Secret Evidence Repeal Act currently before Congress will eliminate the use of secret evidence in deportation hearings conducted by the Immigrations and Nationalization Service."[45]

The use of secret evidence violates the basic right to due process and a fair trial. Racial and religious persecution is offensive to human dignity. Family members are often subjected to harassment as a consequence of a family member facing deportation based on undisclosed information from unidentified accusers. Secret evidence proceedings are discriminatory in practice.[46]

According to the American Civil Liberties Union (ACLU), "No person should be deprived of liberty on the basis of evidence kept secret from the person." Secret evidence violates a fundamental requisite of a fair legal system. "Star Camber proceedings conducted out of right of the accused and her attorney are a feature of totalitarian governments, not of our own. The Supreme Court has said time and again that deportation is a severe deprivation of liberty – one that can separate a person from home, family, career, and all that makes life worth living."[47]

Disturbingly, the ACLU revealed, "Virtually every recent secret evidence case that has come to public attention involves a Muslim or a Arab."[48]

Action Items

- Support the enactment of the Secret Evidence Repeal Act
- Develop public policy forums to increase community awareness concerning the discriminatory impact and injustice of secret evidence

43. Arab American Institute, Internet: www.aaiusa.org/policypriorities/index.html.
44. *Ibid.*
45. American Arab Anti-Discrimination Committee,
     Internet: www.adc.org/action/1999/2nov99.html.
46. *Ibid.*
47. *Ibid.*
48. *Ibid.*

JUSTICE ISSUES

proceedings by the INS and other government agencies
- Challenge all racial discrimination and injustice targeting Arab Americans and all others who are racially or religiously stereotyped and victimized

Reparations

The scriptures of the Bible warn us to not be conformed to this world, but to be transformed by the renewing of our minds. This teaches us that the world, its government and systems, represent that which we should not conform to, but we must open out hearts and minds to that which will renew us by reconnecting us to Him Who created us and to Him Who has the power to renew us and reproduce us.

Africa and the Americas have been ruled under white supremacy and racism, out of which came the institution of slavery, colonialism, and the purposeful destruction of our minds and the denial of our basic human rights, self-determination, love, and education. If there is to be reconciliation between the ethnic, racial, tribal and national entities that have violated the rights of each other, there must be truth.

There must be acknowledgment, confession, or repentance and then an act of atonement. And, in this principle of atonement there must be that which repairs the damage that was done. Certainly the present-day government and Whites are not guilty of the institution of slavery, the present-day Africans are not guilty of selling their brothers to Europeans, but each of us has to accept the responsibility to repair the damage that has been passed on to this generation. We, as Blacks, have to accept the responsibility of doing something for ourselves in the way of repairing the damage. All whose fathers have been party to the destruction must accept the responsibility to help to repair the damage. It is only in the act of repair by this present government and its people that forgiveness can come and reconciliation on the basis of forgiveness that will allow human beings to act as human beings.

So, the act of repair, called reparations, is absolutely and vitally necessary in the principle of atonement. This principle of atonement must be accepted universally, for there are tribes in Africa that have offended each other. There are nations in Europe and Asia that have offended each other. There are nations in the Caribbean and in South America, Central America, North America that have offended each other, as well as other ethnic and racial groups. So, the principle of atonement and repair has to be universally accepted because this world has been a world of evil and injustice and all of us have been victims and have victimized. So, to whatever extent we are guilty, we must accept the responsibility to make a difference.[49]

49.   *Statement from The Honorable Minister Louis Farrakhan, Convener of the Million Family March 2000, January 4, 2000.*

JUSTICE ISSUES

Reparations

Commission to Study Reparation Proposals for African Americans Act
(Introduced in the House of Representatives)

HR 40 IH
106th CONGRESS
1st Session

A Bill

To acknowledge the fundamental injustice, cruelty, brutality, and inhumanity of slavery in the United States and the 13 American colonies between 1619 and 1865 and to establish a commission to examine the institution of slavery, subsequently de jure and de facto racial and economic discrimination against African Americans, and the impact of these forces on living African Americans, to make recommendations to the Congress on appropriate remedies, and for other purposes.

Findings And Purpose

THE APPROPRIATIONS COMMITTEE FINDS THAT:

Approximately four million Africans and their descendants were enslaved in the United States and the colonies that became the United States from 1619 to 1865. The institution of slavery was constitutionally and statutorily sanctioned by the government of the United States from 1789 through 1865. The slavery that flourished in the United States constituted an immoral and inhumane deprivation of Africans' life, liberty, African citizenship rights, and cultural heritage, and denied them the fruits of their own labor. Sufficient inquiry has not been made into the effects of the institution of slavery on living African Americans and society in the United States.

Goals

- Establish a commission to examine the institution of slavery which existed from 1619 through 1865 within the United States and the colonies that became the United States, including the extent to which the federal and state governments constitutionally and statutorily supported the institution of slavery
- Examine de jure and de facto discrimination against freed slaves and their descendants from the end of the Civil War to the present, including economic, political, and social discrimination

- Examine the lingering negative effects of the institution of slavery and the discrimination on living African Americans and on society in the United States
- Recommend appropriate ways to educate the American public of the commission's findings
- Submit to the Congress the results of such examination, together with such recommendations

Environmental Justice

African Americans and other poor and oppressed communities share the burden of disproportionate siting and operation of toxic facilities. This disparate treatment is the manifestation of environmental racism and has been substantiated by numerous studies. Not only are people of color adversely affected by pollution, they receive inequitable treatment from the U.S. government. The government has been bought by multi-national corporations in exchange for public policies that protect the interests of polluting industries in their disregard for public health.

There was an outright assault by the 104th Congress on environmental laws and worker-protection fueled by the right-wing and financed by corporations. The North American Free Trade Agreement (NAFTA), World Trade Organization (WTO) and General Agreement on Tariffs and Trade (GATT) allow U.S. corporations to avoid environmental regulations and fair wages for workers. Exposure to toxic chemicals and disparate treatment by U.S. government agencies has created an epidemic of disorders, illnesses and death, including violence and other behavioral disorders, learning disabilities and a general learning curve decline among African Americans and other poor and oppressed communities. Our communities also suffer from a wide range of reproductive and developmental disorders, cancers and other environmentally related diseases.

Environmental Justice Action Items

- Force the U.S. government to intervene and stop disproportionate siting and operation of toxic facilities in African American and other poor and oppressed communities
- Force the Environmental Protection Agency (EPA) and other U.S. government agencies to stop inequitable and unjust treatment of African Americans and other poor and oppressed people
- Ensure vigorous and expanded enforcement of the President of the United States Executive Order on Environmental Justice
- Advocate for the discontinuation of the use of risk assessment to be replaced with a process that considers cumulative and synergistic exposures as well as adverse socioeconomic impacts

JUSTICE ISSUES

- Secure stronger environmental protection for farm workers and other workers
- Advocate for the implementation of a genuine national pollution prevention strategy
- Educate African Americans, Latino Americans, Native American, Asian and Pacific Islanders, Arab Americans, White Americans and other poor and oppressed communities in the areas of environmental industry and sciences
- Obtain compensation and reparations for contaminated communities
- Obtain health care and compensation and health monitoring for impacted communities
- Ensure that contaminated communities be the primary decision-makers with respect to the assessment of health risks, and the allocation of liability and selection of remedial technology
- Ensure the relocation of people in contaminated communities with buyouts for relocation in comparable housing without debt, and ensure cleanup to the satisfaction of contaminated communities which do not need to relocate
- Achieve Super Fund reform, which maintains strict, joint and several liabilities, and guarantees the involvement of impacted communities in the decision-making process
- Provide worker-training in contaminated communities so that impacted residents can benefit from jobs created by clean-ups
- State delegation of federally funded environmental initiatives and responsibilities, including enforcement, should be delegated only to those states with good environment track records
- Ensure that the U.S. government acknowledges that environmental justice for Native Americans includes respect for sacredness of native lands and sovereignty rights with historical treaty and nationhood status
- Force the U.S. to develop policies, research and practices for sustainable development, and stop production of man-made substances that are not biodegradable or cannot be chemically neutralized
- Create a community-driven, democratic, participatory environmental planning and policy making process at the local, state and national level
- Ensure that environmental laws established during the past 20 years be improved and enforced to fully protect the public health

End Toxic Racism[50]

Poor and minority communities disproportionately shoulder the brunt of pollution in this society. Economically unable to escape, many poor people live next to polluted sites, drink contaminated water, and are exposed to increased health risks from hazardous waste.

Background

Race and income are the most significant factors in determining where toxic waste sites are located. Of 64 studies looking at the disparities in the location of pollution, all but one found environmental disparities either by race or income.

Minorities and poor people continue to live in polluted neighborhoods in disproportionate numbers. Sixty percent of African Americans lived near abandoned toxic waste sites in 1987. In 1994, minorities were 47 percent more likely than Whites to live next to these sites.

The Environmental Protection Agency has made efforts to identify and respond to the injustices caused by toxic racism. However, state and local jurisdictions that oversee land use planning must also address these injustices.

Goals

- Ensure that federal agencies minimize the environmental impact of policies and regulations on poor communities
- Support efforts to identify and clean up toxic sites in poor and inner city communities
- Increase outreach, participation and information for poor communities regarding toxic site clean-up

Nuclear Radiation: Environmental Dangers from Atomic Weapons Plants in the United States

On January 29, 2000, the New York Times reported, "After decades of denials, the government is conceding that since the dawn of the atomic age, workers making nuclear weapons have been exposed to radiation and chemicals that have produced cancer and early death."[51]

50   Congressional Black Caucus, *The Agenda: 1997-1999*, 105th Congress of the United States, Washington, D.C. p. 20.
51.   Matthew L. Ward, "*U.S. Acknowledges Radiation killed weapons Workers*," New York Times, January 29, 2000.

JUSTICE ISSUES

Secretary Bill Richardson who heads the U.S. Dept. of Energy affirmed, "This is the first time that the government is acknowledging that people got cancer from radiation exposure in the plants."[52] It is estimated that more that 600,000 people who worked in the atomic weapons industry since the beginning of Work War II, have cancers directly related to their work environment.[53]

The Million Man Family March calls for justice and compensation for the families of the 600,000 persons suffering from this injustice and supports public policy to prevent a recurrence of this tragedy.

52.   Ibid.
53.   Ibid.

Justice for United States Veterans Injured by Agent Orange

United States Veterans and their families deserve respect and support, in particular, those veterans of the war in Vietnam who were exposed to the carcinogen, Agent Orange. According to the United States Department of Veterans Affairs, an estimated 3.1 million veterans served in the Southeast Asia Theater (Vietnam, Laos, Cambodia, flight crews based in Thailand and sailors in the South China Sea).[54] Of that number, 2.6 million veterans actually served within the borders of South Vietnam and the surrounding waters.[55]

From January 1965 through April 1970, Agent Orange was used extensively by the United States military as a herbicide defoliant throughout Vietnam.[56]

Technically speaking, Agent Orange is a reddish-brown liquid compound containing four highly toxic herbicides:[57]

- 2,4,5–trichlorophenoxyacetic acid (2,4,5-T)
- 2,4–dichlorophenoxyacetic acid (2,4-D),
- Cacodylic acid, and
- Picloram

Government scientists revealed that (2,4,5-T) "was contaminated in the manufacturing process with a type of dioxin–2,3,7,8–tetrachlorodibenzo–p–dioxin, also known as TCDD."[58] Dioxin itself is a toxin known to cause cancer after prolonged exposure, especially in persons who have weak immune systems or other chronic health problems.

Families of veterans contaminated from exposure to Agent Orange, in particular, infants and children, also suffer from cancers and other severe health problems directly as a result of a family member's exposure to Agent Orange.

In August of 1999, the United States Department of Veterans Affairs issued the following statement:

> As knowledge has grown from studies of Agent Orange, some latent diseases that may not have become evident in service have

54. United States Department of Veterans Affairs, Internet: www.va.gov/pressrel/99fsao.htm.
55. *Ibid.*
56. *Ibid.*
57. *Ibid.*
58. *Ibid.*

JUSTICE ISSUES

been recognized as service–connected. Based on clinical research, nine such diseases are now on the presumptive list: chloracne, Hodgkin's disease, multiple myeloma, non-Hodgkin's lymphoma, porphyria cutanea tarda, respiratory cancers (lung, bronchus, larynx and trachea), soft-tissue sarcoma, acute and subacute peripheral neuropathy and prostrate cancer. In addition, monetary benefits, health care and vocation rehabilitation services are provided to Vietnam veterans' offspring with spina bifida, a congenital birth defect of the spine. Veteran Affairs presumes that all military personal who served in Vietnam and who have one of the listed diseases were exposed to Agent Orange.[59]

Authoratative sources estimte that there are more than 3,000 children afflicted with the congenital abnormality as a result of thier parent or parents exposire to Agent Orange during the Vietnam War.

Action Items

- Enact legislation to provide expanded health care for the victims of Agent Orange

- Sponsor research to reveal the truth concerning the horrofic impact of Agent Orange on both U.S. Veterans as well as Vietemese whose health status remains severely impacted as a result of Agent Orange

- Develop pubilc policy to assist families who have been negatively impacted from exposure to Agent Orange

59. *Ibid.*

STRENGTHENING THE FAMILY

STRENGTHENING THE FAMILY

Marriage and Family

We cannot write on the Divine Institution of Marriage until and unless we write of the nature of the male and female and how these natures are made to compliment each other.

It is written in the scriptures of the Holy Qur'an that Allah (God) created the male from a single essence and its mate of the same essence and from these two He spread many men and women. What is the essence out of which male and female have been created? That essence is the nature of Allah (God) Himself. Each creature is created by the Creator for a specific purpose. Until and unless we understand the purpose for the creation of male and female we will never understand the Divine Purpose for the institution of marriage.

Allah says in the Holy Qur'an that He created the man (Adam) as His Khalifah or vicegerent. This word Khalifah means one who takes the place of another or one who succeeds another who has died. Since Allah (God) is the Ever-Living, this verse of scripture teaches us that the Creator (Allah) has created the man to stand in His place to act according to His Will.

This again teaches us of the enormous potential of the human being to rule the universe and all therein in the place of Allah (God), the Originator.

The Bible teaches that He created the man and the woman in His image and after His likeness and He gave them power and dominion (ability to rule). He asked them to multiply and replenish the earth, so, inherent in this multiplication is the nature of the male and the female to be attracted toward each other for the purpose of reproduction and continuance of human life; but, multiplication also means using the multiplier, and the multiplicand to produce a product.

The proper relationship between the multiplier and multiplicand is what gives us the product. Product on one level can be a child but on another level it can be a world. The male and the female are by nature created to produce. Any denial of the opportunity to produce is the denial of the nature of the human being, thus, limiting its justification for existence. The two natures, male and female, are created by Allah (God) with the purpose of producing family, tribes, nations and world; governments, systems: spiritual, economic, political, social, cultural and scientific.

The Bible teaches, **And the Lord God said, it is not good that the man should be alone; I will make him an help meet for him**. He did not want the man to be separated, apart, isolated or without a mate. His mate would give him what was necessary to manifest the best that Allah (God) had put within him. So, it is written that He created the woman to be his help meet. This is an interesting word. A man who is non-productive does not need a helper. The woman is made to help the man meet the objective, obligation or duty that Allah (God) has placed on *the man. She is created by Allah (God) to supply him with what he needs to accomplish the Will of Allah (God), and, he is created to supply her with what she needs to fulfill her role and duty to Allah (God) and to him.*

*Allah says in the Holy Qur'an that, "**Men are the maintainers of women**." Again it reads that, "**He created the woman that he (the man) would find peace and quiet of mind in her**." It also reads that, "**Both the male and female are created to be a covering for each other**." A protection for each other as well as to suffice the needs of each other.*

*This is why the Divine Institution of Marriage from the very beginning was to encourage the male and female to commit themselves, first to their duty to Allah (God) in obedience to Him, and then their duty to each other. Marriage then is the process of the unification, not only of two bodies, but two minds, two spirits and two souls that were created for each other. This institution is so sacred in the eyes of Allah (God) that it is written in the scriptures of the Bible, "**Therefore, what God has joined together let not man put asunder**."*

Marriage is so important with Allah (God) that any interference in the process of the unification of male and female who have committed themselves to each other in marriage is a very serious offense. Remember, before there were nations, governments and systems, there was male and female, marriage and family.

Anything that promotes the process of the unification of male and female in the Divine Institution of Marriage is proper in the sight of Allah (God). So, we must look at the education we receive; the religion and its practice; the government, its policies and laws; the economic system and its effect; the scientific and technological advancement that has been made and its effect on marriage and family. The yardstick or criteria by which we measure good; it must first promote the development of the male and female in accord with the nature of their creation; it must promote marriage; and it must protect family.

In order for education to be proper it must develop human beings (male/female) to become producers. The laws that are made in society must be measured against how they affect marriage and family. The things that we as individuals say and do must be measured by the criteria of what is good for human development, marriage and family. With this criteria we can analyze everything that we say, do, make or produce.

If what we say or do does not produce good for the proper development of the male and female in accord with their natures; unity of the male and female in the Divine Institution of Marriage, and the proper development of family, then, we must rethink what we are saying and doing; the laws that we are making, and, the scientific advancement that we have achieved.

All things that are good are family-friendly. [60]

Strong marriages sustain families. Public policy should be both family and marriage-friendly. The actions of government directed by legislation and public policy should encourage the maintenance of marriage rather than foster a national climate where the stability of marriage is viewed with a lowered value.

60. *Statement from The Honorable Minister Louis Farrakhan, Convener of the Million Family March, February 3, 2000.*

The Million Family March supports the sacred institution of marriage. Current societal challenges and strains to the fundamental covenant of marriage are evident in the following facts:

- During the last 30 years, the overall number of families headed by married couples has sharply declined.
- Throughout the United States, the increase in the divorce rate is higher than the rate of marriages.
- Within six months of marriage, half of all newlyweds begin to doubt whether or not their marriage will last; ultimately 60% of American families are in danger of divorce.[61]
- During 1997, in the United States, there were 2,384,000 marriages as compared to 2,244,000 marriages in 1998, a decline of nearly 1400,000. At the same time, births in the U.S. increased from 3,882,000 to 3,946,000. During this time there was a high rate of divorce of existing marriages.[62]

"Marriage is the cornerstone of the family, and the family is the cornerstone of the nation. If God is the cornerstone of your marriage, your marriage will never fail."[63]

Many of the social and economic problems and ills of American society are directly related to the break-up of marriages and the corresponding breakdown of families. According to recent studies, the increasing rate of suicides among teenagers is connected to marriage failure and family disintegration.[64] The Council on Families in America, in a report entitled, "Marriage in America" concluded, "Our society's current topic might be termed managing family decline or ameliorating some of the worst consequences of a divorce culture...the new discussion we propose might be termed recreating a marriage culture."[65]

Action Items

- Establish a National Pro-Marriage and Family Annual Report Card for members of the United States Congress and state legislatures.
- Encourage public policy makers at all levels of government to have periodic briefing sessions with community and religious leaders con-

61. Joong Hyun Pak and Andrew Wilson, *True Family Values*, HSA-UWC Publishing, 1996 New York City, p. 2.
62. National Vital Statistics Reports, Volume 47, Number 21, July 6, 1999, U.S. Department of Health and Human Services, Centers for Disease Control and Prevention, National Center for Health Statistics, Hyattsville, M.D., p. 1.
63. The Honorable Minister Louis Farrakhan, Public Address, Washington, D.C., 1997.
64. Joong Hyun Pak and Andrew Wilson, *True Family Values*, HSA-UWC Publishing, 1996 New York City, p. 2.

STRENGTHENING THE FAMILY

cerning family and marriage stabilization.

- Conduct parenting and marriage workshops, seminars, and conferences for public policy makers.
- Pass legislation to observe a National Marriage Day to enhance the values of marriage and the relationship between strong marriages and stable families and communities.
- Support public policy that discourages pre-marital sex.

65. *"Marriage in America: A Report to the Nation,"* Council on Families in America, The Institute of American Values, March 1995, Washington, D.C., p. 5.

STRENGTHENING THE FAMILY

Education

True education gives us power to remove impediments in the pathway of our progress. That progress is seen in human evolution from the animalistic plane of human development, where we are creatures that feed on and live by desire without concern of what is correct. Then, we learn to put desires in the context of morality and become moral human beings that further evolve and, become one with a divine and perfect reflection of the characteristics of God and become little gods ourselves.[66]

All members of the family, in particular children, must be given an opportunity to learn in a supportive, safe, and productive educational environment. We want equality of opportunity. To deny a child an opportunity to achieve and acquire an education is to deny human rights.

The American educational system is in crisis. The level of illiteracy, the dropout rate, test scores, plans to attend college are all direct signs that the current school system has failed.

It is estimated that 10 to 20 percent of Americans are functionally illiterate. The public schools cannot keep our youth in the classrooms long enough to make them literate. The dropout rate for high school youth has reached 30 percent and of those who return, only 80 percent of 19 to 20-year-olds receive their high school diplomas.

As one examines the dropout rate among youth and relates it to the low wages given to teachers relative to other professionals, it is easy to see that education is not valued in the American society. A proper education is important to the individual's life chances as well as to the quality of the whole society. What options are available for an individual who does not, at a minimum, receive his or her high school diploma? They are minimal. And, given the inability of one to get a good paying job and secure his or her future, what then is his or her hope for the future?

The resulting insecurity, uncertainty and desperation present in these individuals are the key ingredients for crime, poverty, drugs and immoral behavior produced in our society. Improving the education and literacy levels of all American citizens must be a priority item if America's status as a world power is to be maintained.

One of the things that separate man from beast is knowledge. Knowledge feeds the development of the human being so that the person can grow and evolve into a mature individual who is clear of his or her purpose for being. Individuals who are clear of their purpose in life can then become productive individuals within society and contribute their talents to the betterment of themselves and society as a whole.

Education is supposed to be the proper cultivation of the gifts and tal-

66. *Statement from The Honorable Minister Louis Farrakhan, Convener of the Million Family March 2000, January 4, 2000.*

STRENGTHENING THE FAMILY

ents of the individual through the acquisition of knowledge. Knowledge satisfies our natural thirst for gaining that which will make us one with our Maker. So, true education cultivates the human being - mind, body and spirit - by bringing us closer to fulfilling our purpose for being, which is to reflect God. The second purpose for education, after self-cultivation, is to teach us how to give proper service to self, family, community, nation and then to the world.[67]

Policy Recommendations

Teachers must be compensated commensurate with their role in society. Teachers should be given tax credit, which increases with seniority. Increased benefit should be given to those teachers who continue their education in their particular area of instruction. Better benefits to teachers will aid in attracting and retaining our talented intellectuals who are being lured away from community development into corporate America.

It is incumbent upon parents and community leaders to have more statutory oversight concerning administration of schools. Knowledge-based education is preferable to competitive-based education in a society that is multi-racial, multi-lingual and multi-cultural.

There should be public funding for charter schools. These schools can be run by an association of parents, teachers and business leaders or any combination of these who are signatories of the charter.

Community involvement in the education of our youth should be encouraged through the establishment of educational tutoring assistance programs. This program should provide tax credit for individuals who donate a minimum amount of time to a public school to help tutor and train its students. Our elders should be encouraged, as they are the necessary links to our youth, to strengthen the educational process within the community.

Dress codes and/or school uniforms are a way to counter the rampant materialism and sexism in the society at large. Dress codes may minimize class differences and focus attention on learning. Dress codes promote uniformity, brotherhood and sisterhood. Incentives and increased funding, and the like should be used to encourage schools to adopt this operating principle. In addition, teaching courses on self-empowerment and self-improvement will minimize issues with self-esteem, self-confidence and self-discipline.

67.   The Honorable Minister Louis Farrakhan, *A Torchlight For America*, FCN Publishing, Chicago, Illinois, p. 47.

STRENGTHENING THE FAMILY

Tracking

"Racial tracking in education is an insidious form of mis-education and discrimination which uses the pretense of 'ability' to maintain inequalities in public schools by placing children of color and poverty into inferior and separate classes, courses of study and/or schools. It assures the continuing relegation of most children of color and poverty to an inferior, separate and unequal education that destroys or minimizes self-esteem, human potential and ultimately, family growth and stability." The Million Family March will challenge racial tracking in education.[68]

Action Agenda Items

- Encourage church involvement in education
- Improve the fundamental literacy rate among school children by encouraging businesses and civic organizations to adopt a school and provide reading materials
- Establish Manhood and Womanhood Training
- Organize volunteers from churches, businesses and civic organizations to read to students during the day and tutor them to improve their reading and writing skills
- Examine school and public libraries in communities
  ° Insist that libraries order books which reflect the ethnicity of the community
  ° Insist that libraries carry books in technology, science and current events which are reflective of Black American, Latino American, Asian and Pacific Islander and Arab American accomplishments and their current involvement in these fields
  ° Increase the number of African Americans, Latino Americans, Native Americans, Asian and Pacific Islanders, and Arabs in the states' teacher corps, particularly males, by encouraging them to enter education and teacher-training programs in college
- Develop a "hiring web" reflective of minority educators who are certified teachers, administrators and other skilled support staff (such as social workers, school psychologist and guidance counselors) who are seeking employment opportunities
- Focus on early intervention and pre-school programs. Either establish or increase the availability of these programs
- Develop "parent centers" within each school system at a central loca-

68.   Rose Sanders, Esq., Statement on Tracking, January 4, 2000, p. 3.

tion which will establish a resource of information on parenting, covering such issues as:

- ° Child care
- ° Health and immunization
- ° Parental rights
- ° Special education
- ° Formal discipline (expulsion)
- ° Educational development
- ° Skill mastery and aptitude level outlines

- Develop "College Experience Tours" with colleges and universities that have a tradition of serving the educational interests of our communities, whereby students at the middle school level visit and stay at a college for a week with a student volunteer and are shown what is possible with determination and support. This practical experience can do several things, i.e. improve our youths' self-image and foster the economic funding of colleges and universities which serve the interests of our communities
- Evaluate problem-solving methodology vs. memory-based learning
- Establish study groups in communities on the Million Family March
- Prioritize math and science in school curriculums for all students
- Eliminate all racial and cultural bias in standardized testing
- Require Internet access for all schools
- Constitutional Rights and meaning of Fourteenth Amendment for all disenfranchised persons and groups
- Equal distribution of resources and technology to schools
- Require 18-year-olds and younger to attend school
- Abolish racial tracking in schools
- Protect athletic fairness and equal opportunity in higher education
- Challenge all forms of social inferiority institutionalized in educational systems
- School curriculums should include values of love, respect, collective responsibility, and community-focused leadership
- Encourage parental involvement in the total life of the child
- Support community campaigns for Replacing Inequities in our Schools with Excellence (R.I.S.E.)
- Core school curriculums should include math, science and the arts for all students and the study of self and one's environments
- Support teacher-sensitivity training and adequate compensation for careers in teaching
- Support multi-ethnic and cultural studies
- Teach basic economics at the earlier stages of development

Education: Rehabilitate Our Schools
and Improve Access to Education[69]

All children must be given an opportunity to learn in a supportive and safe environment. Schools are collapsing, educational potential is being stifled and financial barriers deny children access to higher education.

Background

Our elementary and secondary schools face problems of overcrowding, crumbling buildings and other significant maintenance problems.
- Over 60 percent of these schools desperately need repairs.
- The average urban school needs $1.7 million to repair and upgrade its facilities to acceptable conditions. The price tag for the repairs nationwide is estimated to be $112 billion.

Higher education is also out of reach for many of our students because of financial barriers.

- Since 1980, the Pell Grant program for needy students has not kept pace with college costs. In real dollars, appropriations for the program have increased by only 49 percent, while college costs have increased by 230 percent.
- Historically Black Colleges and Universities (HBCU), where 28 percent of African American students receive their undergraduate degrees, are now fighting for survival because of funding issues and legal challenges.

While President Clinton has proposed several initiatives on education, they do not go far enough to make education affordable and accessible for poor and minority students.

Goals

- Support a $20 billion school infrastructure capital outlay program to rebuild, repair, and improve our elementary and secondary schools
- Increase the maximum Pell Grant award to make college more affordable
- Support funding for and legal status of Historically Black Colleges and Universities
- Expand President Clinton's educational proposals

69. Congressional Black Caucus, *The Agenda: 1997-1999*, 105th Congress of the United States, Washington, D.C., p. 6.

Education From The Perspective of Latino Americans[70]

100,000 NEW TEACHERS

The Congressional Hispanic Caucus strongly supports the administration's commitment to assist local school districts to hire more qualified teachers to teach in our public schools. The aging of the teaching population is creating shortages of qualified teaching professionals to work in our nation's schools. Institutions located in urban areas have a harder time attracting qualified teachers from the dwindling available pool. According to Census estimates, by the year 2030, Hispanic American students ages 5 to 18 will number 16 million and comprise 25 percent of the student population. Coupled with this fact is the reality that a significant proportion of Hispanic American children will also grow up in poor households. This will provide critical challenges to our nation's policy makers as they seek ways to eliminate poverty and low education attainment. We must start securing the necessary resources that will serve to prepare them for the future. This includes an adequate supply of teachers.

SCHOOL MODERNIZATION/CONSTRUCTION

The CHC strongly supports urgently needed funding to help repair and rebuild America's schools. Schools located in urban areas normally have a high concentration of low-income students and tend to have the oldest school structures desperately in need of repairs and upgrades. In order to accommodate the growing number of students attending our nation's public schools, we must ensure that districts serving high numbers of low-income students are given priority in receiving federal assistance for school construction. The CHC supports providing tax credits of zero percent interest for 15-year school construction bonds issued by states and local school districts.

ELEMENTARY AND SECONDARY EDUCATION ACT (ESEA)
REAUTHORIZATION

The administration must vigorously defend ESEA which includes critical funding for many programs aimed at serving the Latino American student population. The education crisis of Latino Americans is a national problem. To tackle this crisis, new and existing education programs must address the Latino American education gap as well as improve the quality of instruction and condition of schools overall.

70. Congressional Hispanic Caucus, *Legislative Priorities: 1999*, 106th Congress of the United States, Washington, D.C., p. 1.

STRENGTHENING THE FAMILY

- Bilingual Education - The Caucus strongly opposes limits to Limited English Proficiency (LEP) instruction. The CHC supports greater accountability measures to ensure adequate instruction, training and a system to appropriately measure bilingual students' progress. Additionally, the CHC will support the administration's increase of $35 million for FY2000 LEP teacher training and certification.

- Title I - This program, the largest federal education grant to states, focuses on poor or disadvantaged students in grades K-12. Thirty-two percent of Title I students are Hispanic Americans. The CHC recommends evaluating changes to the funding formula during ESEA reauthorization to ensure a fair allocation of resources. It will also press for the Department of Education to design strong account-ability measures for Title I funds.

- Migrant Education/Hispanic American Employment Program (HEP)/CAMP - The CHC applauds the administration's recommen-dation to increase funding for these programs, 67 percent for HEP ($6 mil.), 75 percent for CAMP ($3 mil.) and 10 million dollars for a new Migrant Farm worker Youth program. The Caucus will actively work with the administration and others in Congress to secure these program funds which are critical to migrant families.

- Adult Education/English as a Second Language (ESL) - Provide resources to ensure that all who desire to learn English have access to programs which serve them. The CHC supports current proposals to include a new tax credit for employers to provide ESL instruction to its employees.

LATINO AMERICAN DROPOUT

The highest dropout rate of any ethnic group is amongst Latino Americans at 33 percent. Moreover, Limited English Proficient (LEP) stu-dents dropout at a rate of 50 percent. The CHC will work to reduce the Latino American dropout rate. Specifically, the Caucus will request that the Department of Education maintain statistical information on dropout rates for elementary and secondary schools for all ethnic and gender groups.

- Social Promotion - The CHC will actively encourage state education agencies/local education agencies to eliminate social promotion prac-tices (moving a student to the next grade level whether or not he or she passed the previous grade). However, it will also call for these agencies to enact strong accountability measures to improve class-room practices to ensure that students do not to repeat the same experience that led to failure in the first place.

HISPANIC EDUCATION ACTION PLAN (HEAP)

The success of the administration's Hispanic Education Action Plan will require a concerted effort by the Department of Education to ensure that it reaches the targeted communities. The proposed $520 million for FY2000 will have a real impact on the Latino American community only if the dollars reach the community. The Caucus will urge the administration to develop a specific implementation plan to guarantee that these funds not only reach intended communities, but also include:

Data Collection: It is imperative that the Department of Education collect data that will show the participation of Latino Americans in each program. This information will provide a definitive answer of whether or not Latino American participation increased with increased funding.

Performance Measures. Performance measures are critical to measure the effectiveness of each program in providing intended services to the community.

Oversight. The Department of Education should designate a senior official within the agency to oversee the implementation of HEAP.

Special Education

The Impact of Labeling Students with Special Needs[71]

THE PREMISE

The number of students labeled as "Students with Disabilities" or "Students with Special Needs" has steadily increased over the years. Mislabeling of some students can lead to their inappropriate education and leave them ill-prepared to function in society.

As referenced above, in his book, *Torchlight for America*, the Honorable Minister Louis Farrakhan defined the purpose of education. He wrote, "Education is supposed to be the proper cultivation of the gifts and talents of the individual through the acquisition of knowledge."

The federal law which governs the rights of individuals with disabilities is called the Individuals with Disabilities Education Act (IDEA), commonly referred to as IDEA '97. Part B of the act, Amendments of 1997, §300.26 (a) (1) defines special education as specifically designed instruction, at no cost to the parents, that meets the unique needs of a child with a disability, (i) the instruction could be conducted in the classroom, in the home, in hospitals and institutions, and other settings. (ii) instruction could include physical education, (which encompasses physical therapy and motor development).

There is an alarming trend which involves assessment and placement of students in special education programs when it appears that alternative programs in regular education settings might better meet their needs. To cite an example, total student enrollment in the Washington, D.C. school system is over 70,000. Currently there are over 10,000 students enrolled in special education programs. Regular education programming alternatives include:

- Smaller classroom settings
- Individualized instruction
- Remedial academics and tutoring
- One on one instruction and counseling as necessary

Instead of incorporating these and other educational strategies in the regular educational setting, many students are referred for special education instruction. Those students are then referred to as "Students with Disabilities" or "Students with Special Needs".

§ 300.13 of IDEA defines the term, free appropriate public education

71. Sister Ruth Muhammad, Special Education Administrator, Washington, D.C., January 4, 2000.

(FAPE), as special education and related services that: (a) are provided at public expense, under public supervision and direction, and without charge; (b) meet the standards of the SEA, including the requirements of this part: (c) include preschool, elementary school, or secondary school education in the state; and (d) are provided in conformity with an individualized education program (IEP) that meets the requirements of §300.340-§300.350. While federal law (IDEA '97) mandates that students who require assistance in education have a right to a free and appropriate education at no cost to the parent, that child also has a right to be educated in the least restrictive environment. According to IDEA, § 300.500, the general requirements for the least restrictive environment means the public agency shall ensure: (1) that to the maximum extent appropriate, children with disabilities, including children in public or private institutions or other care facilities, are educated with children who are non-disabled; and (2) that special classes, separate schooling or other removal of children with disabilities from regular educational environment occurs only if the nature of the severity of the disability is such that education in regular classes with the use of supplementary aids and services cannot be achieved satisfactorily.

Students evaluated as having a visual impairment, hearing impairment (including deafness), or an orthopedic impairment, can with appropriate evaluations, be more easily identified and placed in the appropriate educational environment. As a result, one can more readily justify why a student with one or more of the previous disabilities might require educational programming in a special educational setting. However, when labeling students with disabilities such as emotional disturbances, specific learning disabilities, and mental retardation, the resulting educational programming can translate into an educational injustice to our children. In an effort to provide a "better education" in smaller settings, some educators, advocates, evaluators, and parents opt for or promote assessment and placement of students in full-time special educational settings. The education system, both regular and special, needs to re-examine this practice. All students should be prepared to become productive members of society. They should be taught to use their potential to the greatest extent possible, depending on their individual ability, and then be provided the opportunity to transform that potential to reality. The lack of appropriate programming for students has led to a high referral rate of students for special education assessments, resulting in their mislabeling and placement in restrictive or segregated educational settings. Once labeled, many of our students continue their entire educational process in restrictive or segregated settings. They often do not experience substantive interaction with their non-disabled peers during the school day, in spite of the fact that many of these students can be observed experiencing social interaction on the weekends in churches, community activities, or family gatherings. Education in more restrictive environments decreases their chances of receiving an appropriate education, and sometimes, a high school diploma. Chances for gainful employment upon completion of their education are diminished, due to lack of appropriate training and exposure to opportunity. As a result of inadequate preparation, these students are unable to successfully compete in society.

Solution

As a community we have to assess our students abilities, not just their disabilities. It is the responsibility of everyone involved in their education, to ensure that students are educated in the least restrictive environment. This includes all of the policymakers, educators, advocates/attorneys, administrators (of both regular and special education programs), professionals who assess and place students, as well as the parents. The least restrictive environment should be a regular education program, if at all possible. In the event it is determined that a student's needs cannot be satisfactorily met in a regular educational environment, then support needs to be put in place to supplement the student's educational program. Support, such as smaller classroom settings, tutoring, individualized instruction, and remedial classes, should be implemented before referring a student for special education assessment. If it is determined that a student cannot achieve success, even with support, then special education programs should be incorporated. Initially, the least restrictive educational setting should be attempted, allowing the student to be educated in an environment with his or her non-disabled peers. Should such an attempt fail, the students should then be placed in a full-time or more restrictive setting.

This is not to say that all students who are assessed and placed in full-time special education settings are inappropriately placed. Some students require a more restrictive educational setting to meet individual needs. However, parents, educators, and advocates need to ensure that all students receive instruction in the most appropriate setting and that special education is not a repository for those students whom we have failed to develop comprehensive programs for in the regular educational setting. Failure to do so is an injustice to the students, their families, and to society.

Remember, one of the goals of education is to teach us how to give proper service to self, family, community, nation, and then to the world. One cannot accomplish this unless he or she has been properly educated in the least restrictive environment possible that reflects society in general. The ultimate goal is to produce an individual that is a productive member of society.

Our youth must be developed as leaders both for today and for the future. Leadership training programs and active participation in community development should be encouraged. A detailed agenda on this subject must be developed. The process has begun and must receive priority.

The issue of leadership from a youth's perspective[72]

If THE NATIONAL AGENDA 2000-2008 is to become more than a program of ideas and words, then we must have strong and effective leadership. In fact, one of the goals of the national agenda must be the selection, development and implementation of effective community-focused leadership.

Leadership is naturally the difference between activity, which goes in circles and leads nowhere and activity that is expected, focused and productive.

Too often the leadership in our communities have lead us to dead ends, stagnation and even self-destruction. Leadership has no moral tone. Excellence in leadership can be used for moral and immoral goals and purposes in our communities; we have excellent "gang leaders." That same energy can be directed or reharnessed to uplift families and communities.

Our challenge is to develop community-focused leaders with vision, purpose and commitment to principles of peace and justice for all people. Self-focused leadership is divisive and dangerous.

There must be a deliberate and systematic effort to develop positive family, youth, and political, economic, spiritual and educational leadership to fulfill the promise of the Million Family March. Strong family leadership will help deliver the leadership required to fulfill the community-focused leadership needs of the new millennium.

The leadership to implement the national agenda requires the following policies and practices:

- Educate families on the value of leadership and fellowship.
- Select leadership based upon our needs rather than selecting leaders from among those who push themselves forward for positions.
- Urge every organization to have a strong youth leadership component.

72. Statement from Malika Sanders, Executive Director of 21st Century Youth Leadership Movement, Selma, Alabama, January 5, 2000.

STRENGTHENING THE FAMILY

- Understand that values and leadership are always inter-wound; part and parcel of each other and that if we want community-focused leaders we must have community-focused leadership development programs.
- Establish continuing leadership development in every organization.
- Establish leadership development courses for all students from early education through college.
- Teach our people that leadership is not tied to position but to action with or without position.
- Strategize a process and principles of accountability that will give families and citizens a forum to evaluate and hold accountable leaders selected or elected to serve them.
- Support and encourage the development of programs that redirect and train gang leaders and "criminal" leaders to address and help implement THE NATIONAL AGENDA 2000-2008 in their personal lives and in their communities.
- Recognize and support effective community-focused leadership, especially youth leaders.
- Encourage community-focused leadership development in every institution and organization that purports to serve our communities and insist that all genders and age groups be allowed and encouraged to develop their leadership potential.

To sponsor leadership-training institutions and programs which enlarge the capacity to build monuments and institutions that uplift family and communities. To encourage local and state political organizations to only endorse candidates for office who have completed a course of training in community-focused leadership and accountability. To encourage national civil rights and political organization to establish a national community-focused leadership training institute.

If these principles and actions are implemented in every sector of our society, we will have the leadership power to fulfill the goals and objectives of each agenda area of the Million Family March. Strong family, political, economic, education, and spiritual leaders are needed to achieve sustained victory.

Teen Pregnancy: Provide Education and Prevention[73]

America can no longer ignore the reality of babies having babies. By virtually every measure, teenage parents and their children will face additional hurdles to succeed in life. We must provide young people with more opportunities so that they can make better life decisions.

73. Congressional Black Caucus, *The Agenda: 1997-1999*, 105th Congress of the United States, Washington, D.C., p. 23.

Background

Approximately one million teenage girls become pregnant each year, with over half of them giving birth. In 1994, one in ten African American teenage girls gave birth. These teenagers, who are increasingly single and poor, have limited academic skills and little hope for success.

Not surprisingly, children born to teenage mothers face more hurdles in life. According to the Children's Defense Fund, these children are more likely to be born with low birth-weight, grow up without fathers, live in less supportive homes, suffer abuse and neglect, spend time in foster care, suffer academically, become teenage parents themselves, and serve time in prison.

In addition to the social costs, teen pregnancy costs the country between $13 and $19 billion each year in added health care, welfare and other costs.

Goals[74]

- Support federal, state and local efforts to educate our young people of the risks associated with teen pregnancy
- Support and promote effective teen pregnancy prevention programs
- Support efforts to solve underlying problems which lead to teen pregnancy, including poverty, low self-esteem and low academic achievement

74. *Ibid.*

STRENGTHENING THE FAMILY

Computer Literacy

Increase Access to Information Technology[75]

Information technology is the bridge to the 21st Century. As our reliance on technology increases, poor and low-income individuals without access to those resources will be left behind.

Background

Many of our children are not being prepared to compete in the increasingly technology-based economy.
- The Department of Labor estimates that 75 percent of all new jobs today require technological skills.
- By the year 2005, computer-related fields will be one of the fasted growing segments of service-industry jobs added to the economy.
- Only 14% of African Americans and 13% of Latino Americans have computers at home, compared to 40% of Whites with computers at home.

Goals[76]

- Ensure comprehensive computer training for all ages and skill levels
- Create grant programs for public private partnerships to establish community computer centers in poor and low-income communities
- Integrate federal efforts such as the Technology Learning Challenge Grant program and the Technology Literacy Challenge Fund to assist with start-up and maintenance costs of community computer programs

---

75. Congressional Black Caucus, *The Agenda: 1997-1999*, 105th Congress of the United States, Washington, D.C., p. 7.
76. *Ibid.*

STRENGTHENING THE FAMILY

Throughout this agenda document, emphasis is placed on the role of the family. Both the traditional and the extended family must be strengthened. Non-traditional families should be embraced so long as the concept, definition and characteristics are consistent with righteousness and morality.

Caregivers: Support and Protect
Grandparents and Other Family Caregivers

Children are losing their parents to drugs, HIV/AIDS and jail. Grandparents, often at great personal sacrifice, must now raise their children's children.[78]

Background

In many instances, family caregivers, many of who are poor and elderly, are the last hope for keeping children off the streets and out of foster homes. However, the new welfare legislation's mandatory work participation requirements and time limits on benefits will make this more difficult.

- Almost 40 percent of the children in a family member's care live with families who have incomes below the poverty line. The poverty line for a family of four is $15,569 annually.
- Thirty-eight percent of grandparent caregivers are African American.
- Eight percent of African American children live with a family caregiver without a parent present, compared to 1.8 percent of White children.

In a recent report prepared by the National Association of Black Social Workers, Inc., kinship care has been a significant informal support system in our culture for many years. Traditionally, families have depended upon other family members and neighbors to help in times of need. The placement of children who are in need of out-of-home care with relatives has been steadily growing in recent years. Much of this growth has been attributed to the increasing number of birth parents who are unable to care for

77.   National Association of Black Social Workers, Inc., *Caregivers: Support and Protect Grandparents and Other Family Caregivers, January 3, 2000.*
78.   Congressional Black Caucus, *The Agenda: 1997-1999*, 105th Congress of the United States, Washington, D.C., p. 5.

STRENGTHENING THE FAMILY

their children due to substance abuse, HIV/AIDS, homelessness, physical and mental illness and incarceration. California, Illinois and New York reportedly represent the states with the largest number of children in kinship care.

The most recent figures indicate that approximately 3.3 million children under the age of 18 live with their grandparents or other relatives. We must be mindful of the fact that most of these families are not involved in the child welfare system. African American grandmothers are the primary caregivers for the children who enter into the kinship care system.

Kinship care is a natural response to a national problem for children in out-of-home care. There has been a growing recognition of the benefits of kinship care and the stabilizing effect the extended family can have on placement. This change has been influenced by the enactment of "federal laws and judicial decisions that help facilitate agencies" provision of the "least restrictive," culturally appropriate placements for children and the much needed services to the children and their caregivers. With the passage of the Adoption and Safe Families Act of 1997, there is considerable pressure regarding shortening the length of stay in care and finding "permanent" homes for children.

Issues

Kinship care is a growing phenomenon across the country and presents many challenging practice and service-delivery issues.

The issue of permanency is not a significant one for many children and families in kinship care because grandparents often feel that the children "belong to them." Many times, the children have been an on-going part of the grandparents' lives.

Often grandparents are reluctant to adopt their grandchildren. Many are rather ambivalent about getting involved in the judicial proceedings of termination of parental rights so that the children can be adopted.

Relative caregivers often experience being in an estranged relationship with the child welfare system. In many instances, children are placed with relatives without support or services. Under the current laws and practices, relatives have no legal rights unless they adopt or obtain legal guardianship.

Caregivers are often unable to access resources and services that are available to traditional foster care families. Financial assistance is often not available unless they are able to access Temporary Assistance for Needy Families (the old Aid to Dependent Families with Children).

Currently, the foster care regulations are governing kinship families. These standards were promulgated to regulate children living with strangers, not family members.

Children should not linger in foster care. However, the Adoption and Safe Families Act presents significant conflict with timeframes. Many of the children come into kinship care as a result of neglect that is attributed to substance abuse by birth parents. Based on the nature of the drug problem, treatment will probably take longer than the initial 12-month period that is the timeframe for beginning the process for termination of parental rights.

Goals[79]

- Advocate for the development of state welfare programs which meet the special needs of grandparents and other family caregivers
- Expand federal support for grandparents and other family caregivers

NABSW Action for Consideration

- The adoption of federal legislation that provides financial support and resources for relative caregivers. Currently, states are reimbursed for foster care and adoption.
- The enactment of subsidized guardianship without termination of parental rights. Possibly exploring joint custody with birth parents and relative caregivers.

79.   *Ibid.*

STRENGTHENING THE FAMILY

STRENGTHENING THE FAMILY

QUALITY OF LIFE

QUALITY OF LIFE

Real health insurance comes from the diet and eating that which was unclean to eating that which is clean. That which is sanitary is that which is clean and that which is unsanitary is that which is unclean. What is the relationship between sanity and sanitarium, insanity and unsanitary? When you put that into the principle of justice, the more deprived of justice human beings are, the more insane or unclean they become. When you can live in filth then you encourage rats, cockroaches, flies and all things that are carriers of disease. So, one of the first things that the Honorable Elijah Muhammad enforced upon us was cleanliness and he said one day that he would like to form a committee of cleanliness to enforce cleanliness in the society. He said cleanliness is not next to Godliness; it is Godliness. So, just helping our people to see the need for, and to get involved in the practice of being clean, will start them on the road to health and sanitary conditions

We were required to take a hot bath or a shower everyday. We were required to put the best foods in our stomachs and therefore the Muslims countenance literally glowed. We never had prescription drugs in our bathroom cabinets. We hardly ever had a headache. We suffered from diabetes but we knew how to master it. The key is not forcing government to give health care to the people. The key is providing the people with an internal force of enlightenment that allows the people to give basic health needs to themselves and, what the government does is to provide people with health care should they need it. But, if you are clean and you eat the proper foods and you try to take control of your thoughts then you are giving sane, and sanitary conditions to yourself and no matter what the government does or does not do, we give health to ourselves by what we do.

The government said it was OK to drink alcohol. God said no and we stopped. The government said it was all right to smoke. God said no and we stopped. The doctors said eat three meals a day. God said no. We ate one meal a day and we got away from the forbidden swine and shell food that is improper. These are instructions to the people because what we represent is empowerment to the masses by giving the masses the knowledge of how to do for themselves rather than to depend on government, but the unity of the masses will give us the power to redirect government.[80]

Health is central to a high quality of life. Good health requires both preventive measures and curative programs. Central to preventive measures is healthy food and healthy eating. Health is not simply the absence of disease, health is defined as a human right.

At the federal level, managed care, social security and Medicare/Medicaid programs are in financial stress. Since medicine is big business and big government, the curative medicine programs contain all of

80. *Statement from The Honorable Minister Louis Farrakhan, Convener of the Million Family March 2000, January 4, 2000.*

QUALITY OF LIFE

the characteristics that challenge our survival, including racism and economic discrimination.

We must change our eating habits. Next, we must reduce the amount of junk food consumed by our children. Cigarette smoking is suicidal, the use of controlled substances also results in illness and death. Poor health contributes to lost income and unemployment.

We must address political issues involving health care with the same critical eye, the same energy and the same demand for equity that we reserve for the most important challenges to our survival.

Health Care

The three leading causes of death among Black people are heart disease, cancer and respiratory illness. Heart disease is the number one cause of death in the United States. In 1992, the death rate from heart disease for Black males was 45.8% higher than for White males. For Black females it was 69.2% higher. Also in 1992, death rates from strokes were two times higher for Blacks than for Whites.

Breast cancer is the second leading cause of death among women in the United States. Cervical cancer is also a serious problem. Black women are more likely to die from this disease than White women. Black men are twice as likely to die from prostate cancer than White men.

Action Items

Increase the level of awareness about risk factors related to heart disease and stroke by collaborating with local community groups to develop a health component that will develop and implement educational activities tailored to meet the needs of the community.

Increase access to awareness and to promote adequate and affordable medical insurance coverage that will ensure early detection and treatment of service for Blacks and other minorities by supporting legislation to increase insurance portability and eliminate pre-existing conditions clauses. Also, mobilize grassroots organizations to support legislation prohibiting insurance or employment discrimination based on genetic testing or information.

Issue: Dismantling of the Health Care Infrastructure

Policy decisions during the past 20 – 25 years, based on cost reduction, have gutted America's infrastructure. There has been a net loss of hospital beds, clinics and availability of health care. Forty-three to sixty million people are uninsured. Privatization of health care has victimized Black and other poor communities. Politicians have abdicated their responsibility. Excess death rates are soaring. Preventable illness is resurgent due to cost cutting. Support for concerned community-based doctors is paramount. On the rise is food contamination by way of chemical additives during the production process.

Issue: Health Parity[81]

The net disinvestments and down-sizing of health care infrastructure increases the gap in health care outcomes. Black, Latino American and other Americans need more, not less, investment to produce more doctors, nurses and dentists. There is also a need for more medical schools, hospitals, and clinics.

Health Care: Improve Access In Poor Communities

Everyone should have access to basic health care. Minorities continue to suffer and die disproportionately from treatable diseases.

Background

African Americans and other minorities disproportionately suffer from preventable and treatable diseases. For example, African American men die from strokes at almost twice the rate of other men, and have a higher incidence of prostate cancer than any other group.

While the overall death rate due to breast cancer has declined, it has increased for African American women. In addition, African American infants are twice as likely as White babies to die before their first birthday. Diabetes also is more common among African Americans than Whites, with the highest rate among African American women.

The lack of access to preventive care and inadequate treatment when care is provided account for the disparate impact on minorities' health. Indeed, almost 31 percent of minority adults do not have any health insurance, compared to 14 percent of White adults. Minorities are twice as likely to have very little or no choice in where they obtain health care. They are also less likely to be satisfied with the quality of their care when they are fortunate enough to receive it.

Goals[82]

- Provide universal health care for all children

81. Congressional Black Caucus, *The Agenda: 1997-1999*, 105th Congress of the United States, Washington, D.C., p. 26.

QUALITY OF LIFE

- Expand community health care centers and increase the number of minority health care providers
- Support increased funding to identify and prevent diseases which impact African American and other minority communities
- Increase voluntary, informed participation in research and clinical trials to study the impact of diseases on minorities
- Expand the religious community's involvement in health issues

Health Insurance[83]

Latino Americans are a medically underserved population. In 1997, Latino Americans constituted 34.2 percent of the total uninsured population —or approximately 14.3 million people. The Congressional Hispanic Caucus will support and monitor the administration's initiative to provide access to health care to uninsured workers.

Children's Health Insurance Program (CHIP)

Of the 42 million uninsured people living in the United States, 11 million are children. Latino American children comprise 27.3% (3 million) of the total number of uninsured individuals, while African American children make up 17.6%, and White children 12.3 percent Specifically, the CHC will work to:

- Ensure that outreach programs are conducted in a culturally competent and linguistically appropriate manner.
- Address CHIP's eligibility problems in instances where children migrate between states.
- Advocate at the national level for states to set at 200 percent of the federal poverty level CHIP's eligibility threshold.
- Support legislation to increase CHIP's funding formula for the territories.
- Seek proportional representation in CHIP's advisory committee.

Public Charge

82. *Ibid.*
83. Congressional Hispanic Caucus, *Legislative Priorities: 1999*, 106th Congress of the United States, Washington, D.C., p. 2.

The fear of becoming a "public charge" has deterred eligible individuals from participating in federal assistance programs. Many legal immigrants who are eligible for federal assistance, including American children of immigrant parents, have not participated in these programs for fear of deportation, denial of citizenship or adjustment of the immigration status. Some of these programs include: emergency assistance to alleviate losses due to crop damage, child nutrition, children's health insurance, and job-training. The CHC will work with the administration to ensure clear guidelines stating the possible consequences of immigrants participating in federal assistance programs.

Managed Care Reform

A. "PATIENT BILL OF RIGHTS"
   The CHC will support legislation that:
   - Facilitates access to emergency care to all people.
   - Ensures the privacy/confidentiality of all patients' records.
   - Includes measures of accountability for health care providers to monitor adequate service to minorities.

B. ACCESS TO SPECIALISTS
   - Raise awareness of health care needs of minority communities not being addressed by managed care, including access to specialists. For instance, minority communities that suffer disproportionately from diabetes and cancers must have access to the appropriate medical treatment.

C. RESTORATION OF BENEFITS FOR LEGAL IMMIGRANTS
   - Support legislation that restores SSI, Medicaid and food stamps to legal immigrants.

Medicare Reform

   - Advocate for the inclusion of prescription drug coverage for all plans and not limit it to Medicare HMOs.
   - Support the expansion of eligibility to adults younger than 65 years old.
   - Advocate for Medicare reimbursements to health care providers in all the territories at a rate similar to that enjoyed by health providers in the states.

QUALITY OF LIFE

Long-Term Care

- Support the $1,000 tax credit to compensate for formal and informal long-term care for people of all ages with three or more limitations in activities of daily living.
- Support the National Family Caregivers Program which would assist families caring for elderly relatives who are chronically ill or disabled.
- Support adult day care programs as an alternative means of providing care for the elderly in our minority communities. With the decrease in payments to many health providers in our minority communities, we must look for alternatives to traditional health care.

Medicaid

Approximately 20 percent of the Latino American population depends on Medicaid for health care coverage. The CHC will:
- Ensure that Medicaid reaches all eligible individuals in our community. One way to achieve this is by conducting culturally competent and linguistically appropriate outreach. Advocate for U.S. territories to receive Medicaid funds under a formula similar to that of the states.

Mental Health

Latino Americans suffer disproportionately from severe depression. Mental and substance abuse disorders come in many forms and include different diagnoses affecting millions of individuals. Of those affected, Latino Americans have been found to have the highest rate of severe depression compared with Whites and other minority communities.

- Support efforts by the administration to educate Americans on the need for quality, affordable mental health care, especially for our minority communities.
- Support parity of mental health issues including drug and alcohol abuse.

Pro Life/Pro Choice

One of the greatest controversies coming out of the political debate in this highly political season is the issue surrounding pro life and pro choice. This is causing great division in politics because of the very, very serious differences of opinion.

As a student of scripture, I am both pro choice and pro life. How could this be? Allah (God) has created everything in nature to obey the nature in which it is created–without deviation. The greatness of the sun, moon, stars and planets have no ability to disobey the law under which they were created.

It is written in the Holy Qur'an that Allah (God) offered this trust to the heavens and they refused it. Nothing in creation wanted the chance to be disobedient to Allah. It is written that man accepted that trust and Allah (God) created the human being as the only creature in the whole of creation that has offered willingly obedience to Allah (God), but has been made in such a way that he can choose to disobey if it pleased him

Inherent in the creation of human beings is the right-of-choice. It is this right, when properly exercised, that brings us into favor with Allah (God), but we have the right to make bad choices and decisions and we must suffer the consequences of our choice and of our decisions. Man and woman had fallen because they exercised the right and chose unwisely. They chose that which ultimately brought about the spiritual death of the human family.

When Moses was sent from Allah (God) to make a nation of obedience to Allah (God), he recognized the right of choice that Allah (God) had given to human beings.

It is written of Moses in these word, 'This day I have set before you two signs: one of life and blessing and one of death and cursing; choose life that you and your seed may live.' In these words of Moses we have both pro choice and an invitation to choose life.

The act of sex is an act that should be entered into by persons who have made a commitment to each other and who understand that this is a responsible act, which then should be followed by the acceptance of the responsibility of life that flows from this act. Certainly, the female has the right over her body to choose to abort the unborn if she desires, but this brings with it a consequence. There is a law in nature that whatever the human being needs, Allah (God) will provide it out of that law to satisfy that need.

Since we are human beings, only humans can be sent to guide, warn, teach, lead, serve, correct and redeem human beings. If we are sick or diseased, a cure will only come through another human being. Whatever the problems are, a human will have the solution. So, to kill the fruit of the womb would be the murder of the answer to our needs and the fulfillment of our most precious desires.

From the time of the passing of Roe vs. Wade, which gave women the right to have an abortion, backed and supported by the United States government, mil-

lions of unborn lives have been destroyed. What has been the consequence of such a choice? Look at the murder rate; the rise in child abuse; abuse of women and violence in the society since we have shown so little respect for human life. This is coming back on us by the coldness that we can see in our children and the heinous crimes that are committed today by young people. The female is the channel through which life comes and if we disrespect life that comes from that channel, then ultimately we would have no regard for the channel itself.

According to statistics recently published, one out of every three women on earth have been sexually or physically abused. We have the right of choice, but we should choose life and blessing and avoid the choice of cursing.

The streets of America today are cursed with violence, death and disease in which we have no cure. We are constantly being afflicted by more and more disease. If we choose a greater respect for life, the God of life will grant us the abundance of life that He promised us.

— Statement from The Honorable Minister Louis Farrakhan, Convener of The Million Family March, February 7, 2000

According to the National Institute of Health Bureau of Health Statistics, since the Supreme Court of the United States ruled in favor of permitting abortion in 1973 in Roe vs Wade, there have been an excess of 35 million abortions performed in the United States. The impact of more than 35 million abortions during this period of time is a matter of great debate and division. Public policy should be based not just on what is politically expedient, but more importantly, public policy should be based on what is right in the sight and presence of God.

Human life is a gift from God. Human life is a blessing from God. No one should have the right to abort or terminate a life that God has created. The Million Family March supports life. The Million Family March supports righteousness and behavior and actions that are right in the sight and presence of God. More than 35 million abortions since 1973 is a grievous and sinful affront to God. The Million Family March supports family, marriage and the preservation of human life.

The value and purpose of life has been lowered and obscured to new depths of callousness since Roe vs. Wade. The womb of a woman is a sacred place where God and woman labor to produce life. Society should not promote abortion. Only in the cases of rape and incest and when the health of the mother is at a severe risk is abortion justified.

Strengthen HIV/AIDS Education, Prevention and Research[84]

Few can claim that they have not been touched personally by HIV/AIDS. Yet, the subject of HIV/AIDS is still taboo in many of our communities.

Background

While the rate of HIV/AIDS infection is decreasing for virtually every other segment in society, it is skyrocketing for African Americans.
- HIV/AIDS is the leading cause of death for African American women and men, ages 25 to 44.
- Contrary to many beliefs, HIV/AIDS is not a "gay disease." Thirty-four percent of African Americans with HIV/AIDS are heterosexual.
- African Americans and Hispanic Americans account for more than 50 percent of all reported HIV/AIDS cases.

Goals[85]

- Reduce the spread of HIV/AIDS in poor and minority communities through increased access to treatment, prevention and education
- Support increased funding for HIV/AIDS education and research
- Encourage faith-based efforts to motivate and maintain a commitment to positive behavioral changes
- Increase outreach, training and technical assistance programs to educate communities on how to access available HIV/AIDS funding.

HIV/AIDS[86]

- In 1997, Latino Americans accounted for 21% of HIV/AIDS cases, but comprised less than 11% of the population. In the same year, HIV/AIDS was the leading cause of death for Latino Americans between the ages of 25 and 44.

84. Congressional Black Caucus, *The Agenda: 1997-1999*, 105th Congress of the United States, Washington, D.C., p. 4.
85. *Ibid.*
86. Congressional Hispanic Caucus, *Legislative Priorities: 1999*, 106th Congress of the United States, Washington, D.C., p. 2.

QUALITY OF LIFE

- Support increased in funding to address high HIV/AIDS incidence in racial and ethnic minority communities.

Tobacco

Latino Americans are disproportionately affected by tobacco-related illnesses. In 1994, lung cancer was the overall leading cause of death for Latino Americans. Latino American men have a lung cancer mortality rate approximately three times that of Latino American women. Furthermore, the smoking rate for Latino high school students increased from 25.3% in 1991 to 34% in 1995.

- Any federal legislation on tobacco should include language to ensure that public health programs in minority communities receive proportional funding.

Department of Health & Human Services (HHS)

The Hispanic Caucus will work with HHS to ensure that its agencies adequately address the needs of the Latino American community. Specifically, the CHC will work to reduce health disparities among ethnic and minority groups in the United States and the territories.

Centers for Disease Control and Prevention (CDC)

- Monitor the CDC's strategies to reduce health disparities among ethnic and minority groups in the U.S. and the territories. The CDC currently runs research/demonstration projects across the country to address six identified areas of health disparity: infant mortality, cancer, heart disease, diabetes, HIV infections, and child and adult immunizations.

Health Care Financing Administration (HCFA)

- Authorize states to cover smoking cessation programs with Medicaid/CHIP dollars
- Ensure that national state programs (Medicare/Medicaid/CHIP) conduct culturally competent, linguistically appropriate outreach to minority communities.

QUALITY OF LIFE

Health Resources & Services Administration (HRSA)

- Monitor the progress of minority health professionals recruitment.
- Work with the Centers of Excellence and the Health Careers Opportunity Programs, the largest minority health professions student recruitment and retention program at HHS, to ensure a more diverse health workforce.

Immunization

- Educate communities on updated vaccinations and their preventive qualities as well as precautions connected with certain vaccinations.
- Educate communities on the use of effects of chemical warfare

Administration for Children and Families

HEAD START
- Increase enrollment of eligible Latino American children to provide them comprehensive health, nutritional, educational and social services.

CHILD CARE
- Ensure that Latino American communities benefit from affordable, quality child care.

CHILD WELFARE
- Ensure funding to state and local programs which protect children by strengthening families and preventing abuse.

Substance Abuse and Mental Health Services Administration (SAMHSA)

- Monitor SAMHSA's HIV/AIDS strategic plan to ensure that health organizations which serve Latino Americans are fairly funded.

National Institutes of Health (NIH)

National Institute for Allergy and Infectious Diseases
- Support increased funding for research into the effects of Sexually Transmitted Diseases (STD) in the Latino American community.
- Research into the numbers of Latino Americans affected by asthma and other respiratory diseases.

QUALITY OF LIFE

NATIONAL INSTITUTE ON ALCOHOL ABUSE AND ALCOHOLISM

- Advocate for a strategic plan to coordinate research on cancer among underserved populations is drafted.
- Ensure that data is collected on disproportionate cancer incidence, mortality and survival rates among ethnic minorities and the medically underserved.

HISPANIC SERVING HEALTH PROFESSIONS FELLOWSHIP

- Secure a research fellowship program to develop Hispanic American health research and training in the health profession targeting Hispanic American students and faculty.

Office of Minority Health, National Center for Health Statistics

- Request accurate data collection of under served sub-populations including Hispanic Americans, Asian and Pacific Islanders, and Native Americans to bolster the HHS Race/Ethnicity and Health Disparities Initiative.

QUALITY OF LIFE

Employment

The issue of employment policy can be viewed in different ways. On one hand, a decent working wage must be supported so that families can survive with one working wage earner. Many families must have available to them, the option of allowing a homemaker who cares for their children as a full-time job. To that end, there must be a public policy that supports this family organization.

On the other hand, we must use discipline and our individual will to make rational choices that allow us to avoid future choices or circumstances that force dependence. We must develop a moral code that realistically helps our young people choose to not have babies as teenagers and to curb behavior that will require them to grow up too fast.

We must choose to parent our young so they stay in school and thereby allow more of them to become eligible for higher paying positions.

We must harness the profit created from our purchasing power to create jobs that serve the needs we identify.

Employment: Increase Training and Job Creation[87]

Most Americans want to get up every morning, work at a decent paying job, and provide shelter and food for their families. Yet, this is out of reach for many low-skilled and poor people in our communities.

Background

Although the new welfare law requires welfare recipients to find employment, many people are unprepared to enter the workforce. Without basic job skills, these potential workers will have few job opportunities.

- Nearly 50 percent of all adults receiving welfare assistance must spend at least 30 hours per week in some sort of work.
- Conservative estimates say 700,000 jobs will need to be created to employ those adults on welfare who will be required to work.
- People of color suffer disproportional disciplinary and discrimination.
- Almost 40 percent of current welfare recipients never graduated from high school and lack literacy skills to perform basic tasks.

87. Congressional Black Caucus, *The Agenda: 1997-1999*, 105th Congress of the United States, Washington, D.C., p. 9.

QUALITY OF LIFE

Goals[88]

- Support direct job-creation through repair and maintenance projects for roads, schools and other public infrastructure projects
- Promote job-creation initiatives which target low-skilled workers
- Support tax credits and empowerment zones/enterprise communities that provide incentives for businesses to hire low-skilled employees

Increase funding for job-training programs for low-skilled and low-income populations should be translated into public policy recommendation at all levels of government.

Latino American Appointments And Federal Employment[89]

POLITICAL APPOINTMENTS

Latino American representation in high-level positions is important to assure that the concerns of our community are incorporated into the decision-making and program development process. Latino Americans represent 7% of Senate-confirmed appointments, 8% of presidential appointments (primarily on boards and commissions), 7% on the non-career Senior Executive Services (SES) positions, and 8% of Schedule C positions.

While the current administration has appointed more Latino Americans than previous presidents, there is still much work to accomplish. The CHC will continue to follow the progress of Latino American appointees and will work with the administration to identify talented Latino Americans to serve as presidential appointees.

LATINO EMPLOYMENT IN THE FEDERAL WORKFORCE

Latino Americans remain the most under represented group in the federal workforce, particularly in high-level positions. Currently, Latinos represent only 6% of the federal workforce, or 4.5 points below the civilian workforce of 10.5 percent. This is more than any other major group. More disturbing is the fact that Latino American federal employment is concentrated in the lower pay levels. Nearly 79% of Latino Americans are employed in the GS-5 to GS-12 positions, while only 2.4% of the career-SES positions are held by Latino Americans.

In addition, Latino Americans are under represented in 16 of the 17 executive departments and 22 or the 23 independent agencies. Most troubling is that departments and agencies with the worst record of Latino American-employment provide services critically important to Latino Americans, including: Commerce (2.6%), HHS (2.9%), Education (3.5%), and State (3.9%). The CHC will continue to follow the progress of how various departments and agencies are implementing OPM's 10-point plan to improve the recruitment of Latino Americans in the federal workforce.

88. *Ibid.*
89. Congressional Hispanic Caucus, *Legislative Priorities: 1999*, 106th Congress of the United States, Washington, D.C., p. 11.

Housing

Housing is a fundamental human right. Homelessness in the wealthiest society in the world is affront to humanity. Family life is to a large measure conditional of the quality of the family's housing.

Public policy makers too often provide legislation remedies on housing that are out of reach for families who have historically been denied equal access to housing opportunities.

The issue of homelessness is a growing social and spiritual crisis in America. In too many cities across the nation entire families live homeless on the streets.

Housing: Expand Affordable Housing[90]

Safe and decent housing is a basic human need. Yet, many of our citizens have no place to call home or cannot afford safe, decent housing.

Background

Today, between two and three million people live on the streets of America. Of that number, almost 40% are children, 24% are families and 24% are psychiatrically disabled. For those poor families who have some form of shelter, over 5 million use more than 50 percent of their income for rent or live in substandard housing. Only 25% of eligible low-income renters traditionally have received federal assistance.

Over the past few years, Congress has consistently cut the budget for housing programs for poor and low-income families. The Department of Housing and Urban Development's (HUD) budget has declined from $26 billion to $16 billion during the 1990s. In the past two years, Congress has slashed programs for the homeless and funds to repair and upgrade public housing. Funds to build new public housing have been eliminated.

Action Items

- Establish Community Development Corporations (CDC)
- Develop funding sources for cooperative housing
- Develop alternative financing programs for new homeowners
- Retain land ownership within the family

90. Congressional Black Caucus, *The Agenda: 1997-1999*, 105th Congress of the United States, Washington, D.C., p. 29.

QUALITY OF LIFE

- Support the call by the Congressional Black Caucus for one million new homeowners
- Support the call by the National Council of La Raza to increase homeownership in under represented Latino American communities[91]
- Provide bilingual housing counseling in markets with significant Latino American populations[92]
- Offer family education on housing and homeownership for all members of the family[93]
- End rental insurance discrimination based on race, color and creed[94]

Goals[95]
- Oppose any efforts to reduce affordable and low-income housing or to eliminate HUD
- Consider a tax credit program to help the middle-class afford housing
- Work with community and union groups to expand low and moderate-income housing

91. La Raza; Internet:www.nclr.policy.net/proactive/newsroom/release.vtml/?id=18283.
92. *Ibid.*
93. *Ibid.*
94. The National Council of La Raza;
     Internet:www.nclr.policy.net/proactive/newsroom/release.vtml?id=1860.
95. *Ibid.*

Welfare Reform

Welfare reform legislation was recently signed which presents a significant challenge to Black American, Latino American and other people, even a significant number of poor Whites. In defense of his actions, President Clinton has stated his intention to offer new legislation in Congress to correct those provisions of the law that were opposed by a broad coalition of groups who rose in defense of the poor. Since any change in the law is uncertain and dependent on the constantly changing articulations of the president's best interest, congressional make-up and temporary interest group coalitions, some attention must be given to the impact of compliance with the law as it now exists.

Jobs, job-training, effective public schools, enforcement of laws against racial bias, universal availability of direct and indirect job-related information, effective affordable transportation are all necessary to any effort to prevent the expected chaos from the welfare reform law. Inefficient institutions are partly responsible for the failure of welfare to serve its traditional charitable purpose. Now that the "safety net" has been removed, we will have to reinforce the ladder and the structure so that people don't fall off and therefore need a safety net to prevent the trauma and pain of hitting the concrete ground of reality toward which we all may fall.

Getting the poor matched with jobs is certainly a worthwhile goal but this goal cannot be achieved without creating other institutions that work. Most jobs are being created away from the neighborhoods where most poor people live.

Transportation must be made available. Many of the jobs are on night shifts, a time when public transit is unavailable and employees offer no transportation or subsidy. Many jobs are subject to the political-social structure of certain ethnic groups and only members and friends of the group have ready access to the job listings. Schools cannot continue to produce students who are unable to complete reasonable tasks associated with entry-level jobs.

In the global marketplace, many jobs are being filled while the entire planet is being looked at as a labor pool. This context allows transnational and less global-minded companies to shop and bid on an expanding number of tasks.

The least amount of conflict comes from a proper balance of the needs of all interest groups. To date, the poor have been discounted as insignificant. But, at the same time, oppressed groups have failed to take responsible action to force traditional institutions to function effectively. Parents must teach, schools must educate and the buses must run on time. Thus, welfare reform legislation must ensure a viable safety net to refortify families.

QUALITY OF LIFE

"The recent changes in federal welfare reform policies and the changes developing in state and local policies have profound implications for the Asian Pacific American community." The harshly restrictive policies toward eligibility of legal and undocumented immigrants will have a disproportionate impact on the Asian Pacific American community given the high number of Asian Pacific American immigrants and non-citizens."[96]

Welfare: Maintain a Safety Net for the Poor[97]

In the zeal to "reform" welfare at any cost, many politicians have ignored the realities of poverty facing our children and families. To think that states will be able to adequately feed, shelter, and provide health care for the poor with less money is wishful thinking at best.

Background

Fourteen million children currently live in poverty. The Urban Institute estimates that the Personal Responsibility and Work Opportunity Reconciliation Act of 1996–will move 2.6 million more people, including 1.1 million children, into poverty. Under the new law, 11 million families, including 8 million with children, will lose income–an average of $1,300 each year.

While most agreed that welfare needed to be reformed, many did not believe that it should be repealed. Yet, the key provisions of the new law essentially repeals safety net programs for the poor. The Act: (i) requires recipients to work after two years regardless of whether or not there are jobs; (ii) imposes a 5-year time limit on benefits; (ii) replaces AID to Families with Dependent Children with capped block grants; (iv) makes dramatic cuts in the food stamp program; and (v) makes certain legal immigrants ineligible for SSI and food stamps.

While the Congressional Black Caucus (CBC) successfully fought to provide health care for many poor children, the impact of the other provisions of the act are still devastating for poor people.

Goals[98]

- Restore the economic floor for needy and disabled children
- Create safe, affordable childcare for anyone who must work under the new law

96. National Asian Pacific American Consortium; Internet:www.napalc.org/content/pro-welfare.
97. Congressional Black Caucus, *The Agenda: 1997-1999*, 105th Congress of the United States, Washington, D.C., p. 22.
98. *Ibid.*

- Provide job-training and create jobs for everyone who needs employment
- Prevent recipients from being penalized for failing to comply with work participation requirements if there are not jobs available

Social Security Reform[99]

Any Social Security reform proposal must include extensive consultation with members of the Congressional Hispanic Caucus at all stages of the policy process. Social Security plays a key role in lifting elderly Latino Americans out of poverty. Specifically, 85.9% of income in Latino American households, age 65 and over, comes from Social Security and only 35% of Latino American families, age 30-50, are covered by private pensions. Latino Americans who have reached 65 years of age have a higher life-expectancy than the rest of the population and thus receive on average an extra three years of benefits.

Any proposal to strengthen Social Security should provide individuals with a solid, guaranteed benefit that lasts for life and keeps pace with the rising cost of living. Reform should not come at the expense of the "social insurance" nature of Social Security, in that the current system protects workers and their families from loss of earnings due to retirement, death, or disability.

Reforms to Encourage Saving by Individuals

Any changes made in the tax code should include mechanisms to encourage saving by low-income individuals. Social Security was not envisioned to be the sole source of income for retired individuals and individual savings is an integral component of sound retirement planning. Unfortunately, due to economic realities faced by many Latino Americans, their private savings are not sufficient to cover the costs of retirement. Thus, proposals to encourage saving should take into account the distinct needs of the Latino American community.

Puerto Rico

Any reform proposal should include provisions that provide the residents of Puerto Rico a safe retirement plan. Residents of Puerto Rico also contribute to the Social Security system through payroll taxes, and deserve a safe and secure retirement.

99. Congressional Hispanic Caucus, *Legislative Priorities: 1999*, 106th Congress of the United States, Washington, D.C., p. 7.

QUALITY OF LIFE

Older Americans have worked hard all of their lives building the American society as we know it today. They come to the end of their work careers to face a life of poor health and poverty. Pension plans that seniors invested in, usually did not keep abreast with the cost of living and inflation trends of the past 20 years. Environmental changes in the air, water and food quality has increased seniors' susceptibility to chronic health ailments like diabetes, high blood pressure, chronic heart disease and arthritis. Medical costs has risen 200% in the past ten years due to changes in health insurance policies and has moved towards a managed healthcare system. Chronic health ailments also force seniors to depend on medications that costs as much as $1,000 per month while most health insurance does not cover 10% of these costs.

Americans have been led to believe that there are basic guaranteed benefits that one receives upon retirement. Retirees believe that their basic life supports of food, clothing and shelter will be provided for with Social Security and Medicare. As a matter of fact, Americans pay a portion of the Social Security and Medicare benefit for the duration of their working life.

Unfortunately, the Social Security administration is practically bankrupt because of the current presidential administration's decision to use Social Security assets to pay off other national debts. Medicare, the emergency health insurance benefit that was established during Johnson era's war on poverty, was never intended to be the primary health insurance for senior citizens. Medicare was designed as a supplemental insurance benefit for the elderly, poor and to cover only certain, specific ailments, not preventative medicine. Congress recently amended the Medicare Bill adding additional coverage like diabetic supplies and annual mammograms, however, the routine doctor visit is still not covered, neither are dental care nor prescription drugs.

As the American society became more mobile, families no longer stayed in one community to live. Seniors who grew up in communities and took care of their own parents, now are left alone as their families moved away to other parts of the United States. Without the extended family structure to care for them, seniors have been forced to rely on assisted-living communities and nursing homes that are also expensive. If a senior can afford additional health insurance (long-term care insurance), the quality of their housing is better than most. However, most seniors cannot afford additional insurance beyond Medicare or Medicaid and must rely on subsidized nursing homes and assisted-living facilities that are grossly understaffed and poorly maintained. The Medicaid system forces a senior to spend down their assets until they are at the poverty level in order to be eligible for Medicaid.

100. Sister Charlene Muhammad, Family Development Specialist, Washington, D.C., January 4, 2000.

QUALITY OF LIFE

Seniors who are forced into subsidized housing facilities are being exposed more and more to abuse and neglect by their so-called caregivers.

Solution

All Americans who have worked to build this nation must be guaranteed a quality of life upon retirement. This includes a living wage in the form of a pension or Social Security and proper health insurance coverage which focuses on preventative health care and therapeutic services.

Seniors who do not have extended families to assist them with daily living tasks, must be provided with assisted-living facilities that are clean, safe, well-managed and can provide the appropriate medical care that is needed.

The elderly must also maintain a strong influential role in the community. Avenues for them to work with children and youth as well as to provide counsel for those who govern would increase their quality of life as well as strengthen the community with their wealth of knowledge and wisdom.

Social Security and Medicare: Protect Our Seniors[101]

Our seniors have earned the right to live their remaining years free from worry about their basic health and welfare needs. Currently, the vast majority of our seniors, many of whom are poor and disabled, rely on Social Security for financial support and Medicare for health benefits.

Background

Social Security and Medicare are important safety nets for many poor seniors. Today, over 38 million Americans receive Social Security benefits. For the 12 percent who live in poverty, Social Security is their lifeline. Without Social Security benefits 42 percent of current recipients would also be forced into poverty. Currently, the Social Security system is funded through the year 2029. While many agree that Social Security needs to be protected for long-term viability, there is disagreement on the steps necessary to accomplish this goal. Today, most of our seniors also rely on Medicare to receive health care coverage. Without it, many could not afford health care.

Goals[102]

- Oppose any effort to privatize the Social Security and Medicare programs
- Fight any attempts to shift program costs to seniors, decrease benefits or reduce access to the programs
- Protect the long-term financing of Medicare and Social Security to keep pace with the inflation rate

101. Congressional Black Caucus, *The Agenda: 1997-1999*, 105th Congress of the United States, Washington, D.C., p. 25.
102. *Ibid.*

Arts and Entertainment

Include minority professionals at all levels of the U.S. entertainment industry

Currently, Latino Americans are one of the most under represented groups in the entertainment industry-in front and behind the cameras. The Congressional Hispanic Caucus members will meet with industry groups to discuss this problem and their plans to change this trend. We will involve labor organizations (Screen Actors Guild, Writer's Guild and Non-Profits) in these discussions and ask their support in highlighting the enormous economic value Hispanic American actors and their auidences present to the industry.[103]

Recent NAACP agreements with the three major television networks, ABC, CBS and NBC, will create greater opportunities for minorities in all network operations. In a January 7, 2000 statement issued by NAACP, President and CEO Kweisi Mfume emphasized the following:

The NAACP has worked extremely hard with our coalition partners over the last several months to create opportunities for qualified men and women of color. Their ability now to significantly impact executive, production and talent ranks of network television is greatly enhanced.[104]

National Arts Councils and Boards

Minorities involved in the arts are often under represented on national boards and councils dealing with the arts. Greater Minority representation in these oversight groups, especially with those which receive and are charged with distributing, federal funds.

Television News is entertainment: Latinos are very under represented in this medium

Television news has moved from information and analysis to entertainment. Latino Americans must be a proportional part of this medium.

---

103. Congressional Hispanic Caucus, *Legislative Priorities: 1999*, 106th Congress of the United States, Washington, D.C., p. 9.
104. Kweisi Mfume, President, NAACP: Internet:www.naacp.org.

QUALITY OF LIFE

Networks, as well as the FCC, must be held accountable, as operators of the public airwaves, to present an image that is not only positive, but also accurate.

Many rappers and other music entertainers have come under fire for the content of their lyrics, however, music producers, records executives and record companies must also be held accountable for the product which they produce. Following an April 3, 1997 Summit at the National House of the Nation of Islam, music entertainers pledged the following:

> I pledge that from this day forward I shall neither say nor do anything that inhibits or prevents the rise of myself, my family and my people.

> I pledge that from this day forward I shall use my talents and my gifts to promote the liberation of my people and all human beings who suffer from ignorance.

> I pledge that from this day forward I, as a leader, as a teacher, as a guide, as a friend, and as a brother will lead my people to the best of themselves, with the help of God.

> I pledge that from this day forward I will strive to increase my knowledge to increase my faith, to increase my righteousness that I might be a better example for all those who follow me, so help me God.

> I pledge that from this day forward I will never add to the controversy that puts East against West, West against East, brother against brother, sister against sister, but I will use my rap to lift my people's sights to the mountain of justice, peace and true liberation, so help me God.

> I pledge that from this day forward I renounce the hatred of myself and my hatred of my brother. I ask forgiveness for my wrings that have ill-affected my brother, and I ask to be forgiven as I forgive. And I forgive all that have offended me.

> We march as one, as a solid wall of Black unity, African unity, African solidarity, for the spiritual, moral, intellectual, social, economic and political upliftment of our people, so help us God.[105]

105. *The Final Call News*, FCN Publishing, Chicago, Illinois, Volume 16, No. 24.

Action Items

- Protect the artistic and intellectual property of the family
- Promote family-friendly art, culture and entertainment
- Sponsor family day art festivals

QUALITY OF LIFE

QUALITY OF LIFE

ECONOMIC TRANSFORMATION

ECONOMIC TRANSFORMATION

Rebuilding The American Economy

Wall Street reaches new highs almost daily. Yet, many minority populations suffer more and more as the days past. Economic growth in these communities is either stagnated or decreasing. Economic restructuring is desperately needed as both physical and emotional decay has never been greater in our communities.

The American government has continuously called on its citizens to pay higher taxes in order to balance the budget, provide for Medicaid, Medicare and rescue Social Security, yet, we have committed millions of dollars to fight foreign wars.

We cannot wait for the government to recognize the priority of our needs. Money spent on foreign interest can not be used to strengthen the inner-city economies. It is time to change our economic behavior. We have sufficient income to increase our income and wealth simply by changing what we buy, when we buy, and how we buy it. We must circulate money within our own communities.

If we pledge to spend at least 75% of our dollars within our communities, we will create more jobs, more businesses and will create greater economic growth than any government policy can ever deliver.

Action Items

- Redirecting national budget surplus to capitalize economic development in communities that historically are economically exploited
- Encourage family members to engage in international commerce and trade
- Reform U.S. tax code
- Develop cooperative banking alternative to
- Investment funding for public pension, religious funds and philanthropic funds

ECONOMIC TRANSFORMATION

Urban and Rural
Economic Development

Build Strong Communities[106]

There has been a systematic abandonment of America's inner cities and rural communities. To build strong communities, America must invest in jobs, businesses and opportunities in these communities.

Background

Urban and rural America has been deteriorating for decades. Nearly 33 percent of all African Americans and Hispanic Americans living in poor urban and rural areas have incomes below the poverty line. The unemployment rate for African American teenagers approaches 42 percent.

Despite periods of economic growth, many urban and rural communities have never experienced the economic upturns felt in many parts of the country. Poverty engulfs one in every five of America's children.

Budget cuts have devastated federal urban and rural programs across the board. These cuts included programs dealing with housing, job-training, education, transportation and hunger.

Goals

- Develop and strengthen initiatives to create jobs, businesses and other economic opportunities in poor urban and rural communities
- Oppose budget cuts that will harm poor urban and rural communities
- Ensure that economic development programs such as Community Development Block Grants and Section 108 Loan Guarantees reach poor urban and rural areas
- Expand empowerment zones and enterprise communities to assist in

106. Congressional Black Caucus, *The Agenda: 1997-1999*, 105th Congress of the United States, Washington, D.C., p. 28.

rebuilding poor urban and rural communities with particular emphasis on strengthening oversight and accountability toward the interest
of the indigenous residents

Agriculture

Improve Access to Resources for Black Farmers[107]

By the year 2015, it is projected that all African American farms will vanish. With them, economic independence, jobs and tradition will also disappear.

Background

On April 23, 1997, the Congressional Black Caucus (CBC) held a hearing to address the plight of the Black farmer. While most small farmers are struggling to survive, farms owned by African Americans have dwindled dramatically over the past 70 years.

- In 1920, one in seven farmers were African American. By 1982, the number had dwindled to one in sixty-seven.
- Today, there are only about 18,000 African American farmers–less than .01 percent of all farmers. Each day, African American farmers lose 1,000 acres of land.
- Currently, there are over 760 discrimination cases pending at the United States Department of Agriculture (USDA).

Goals[108]

- Support passage of the legislative goals recommended by the USDA Civil Rights Action Team (CRAT) to eliminate discrimination and protect minority farmers
- Eliminate the backlog of discrimination complaints and other participation barriers at the USDA
- Encourage full and equitable funding of USDA loan, technical assistance and other resource programs designed to assist small and poor farmers
- Work with certain land-grant institutions of higher education and other organizations to reverse the trend of land loss and declining participation of minority farmers
- Implement the Fund for Rural America

107. Congressional Black Caucus, *The Agenda: 1997-1999*, 105th Congress of the United States, Washington, D.C., p. 11.
108. *Ibid.*

ECONOMIC TRANSFORMATION

Business and Economic Development[109]

Ensure Adequate Funding for Public Housing

Ensure that the public housing bill passed in the last Congress does not adversely affect public housing residents. Secure adequate funding for public housing within HUD's budget.

Increase the Level of Affordable Housing

Increase the level of home ownership in low and moderate-income communities that will in turn increase community wealth.

Ensure Compliance with the Community Reinvestment Act

Encourage businesses to give back to the community. As financial institutions merge into large ones, it is important that their CRA obligations reflect this evolution.

Technology

Hispanic American business innovations must be fostered in the modern economy, innovation remains largely the work of smaller firms. For this reason, the federal government must maintain its support of research and development efforts by Hispanic American small businesses.

Expand Hispanic American Participation in Federal Research and Development Programs

During FY97 minority and disadvantaged-owned firms received 5,520 Small Business Innovative Research (SBIR) awards, representing 12% of all SBIR awards. With the rise in the number of Hispanic American technolo-

109. Congressional Hispanic Caucus, *Legislative Priorities: 1999*, 106th Congress of the United States, Washington, D.C., p. 9.

gy firms, this percentage should increase as more Hispanic American businesses become aware of the SBIR program and other R & D assistance.

Increase Use of the Internet to Access Latin American Markets

Parts of Latin America are experiencing the fastest Internet growth in the world in terms of users and sites. Thus, to develop valuable business relationships in Latin America, Hispanic American businesses must be competitive with other U.S. firms in their technological capabilities.

Procurement

Discourage the bundling of contracts, which harm small business owners. Streamlining actions by agencies in government purchasing since 1994 have had harmful effects on small firms through bundled contracts. This practice has placed many procurements out of the reach of small firms.

Utilize New Disadvantaged Business Enterprise Regulations

Last year, the Department of Transportation issued new rules for the Disadvantaged Business Enterprise (DBE) program. Among other changes, the new rules alter the way state and local governments set and attain goals for DBE participation. The statutory 10 percent national goal is neither a floor nor a ceiling. Instead, local communities must set their goals based on local evidence of the actual availability of qualified DBEs and use race-neutral methods, such as outreach, to meet as many of their overall goals as possible.

Regulations and Taxes

The intention of SBREFA was to minimize the adverse impact of regulations on small businesses without jeopardizing the legitimate regulatory goals that they are required to purse. SBREFA must be expanded to ease the regulatory burden on small businesses.

Reduce the Tax Burden on Small Businesses.

We must relieve the burden of taxes on small businesses, in particular those businesses that are owned and operated by minority groups that historically, have been economically disenfranchised.

Trade

Exporting can mean big profits for a small business. In light of the broadening market in Latin America, Hispanic American businesses are uniquely positioned to take advantage this new arena of business.

Expand Exports for Global Small Business

Once a small business has decided to go global, utilization of resources and programs that generate trade information is an essential tool for success. Establishing relationships with experienced exporters is also important.

Expand Commercial and Economic Ties for Lenders Seeking New Markets

For lenders seeking to reach a high-growth market, increase profits, reduce risks, respond to clients' needs and invest in their community.

Access to Capital

Hispanic American-owned businesses must have the tools to succeed and compete. This means providing better access to capital and credit. It also means ensuring that federal programs assisting small businesses are responsive to the Hispanic American community. Programs of significance include the 504 Certified Development Company (CDC) Program, the 7(a) Loan Program, and the Small Business Investment Company (SBIC) Program.

New Market Initiatives (NMI)

In his State of the Union address, the president announced that the New Market Initiative is a broad public-private partnership designed to increase business opportunities in underserved urban and rural communities. By creating tax credits, loan guarantee incentives, a network of private venture capital companies, and technical assistance and mentoring programs, the New Market Initiative is designed to make it attractive to businesses to invest in our untapped rural and inner city communities. The initiative will stimulate job-growth, neighborhood revitalization and economic development in the communities that are being left behind.

ECONOMIC TRANSFORMATION

Telecommunications

The telecommunications industry should be more family-friendly. In other words, telecommunications goods, services and profile should not only deliver high-quality at reasonable rates, but also should enhance the transfer of information and equal opportunities for employment, investment and entrepreneurial uplift for families.

The Million Family March supports public policy that advocates independent and alternative ownership of telecommunications systems such as Nation One Communications, a newly established Chicago-based national alternative minority-owned telecommunications company.

Telecommunications: Ensure Access to Technological Opportunities[110]

Telecommunications technology dramatically affects the way we communicate, work and do business. The Telecommunications Act of 1996 provided opportunities for minority and small businesses to play a vital role in the emerging telecommunications industry.

Background

The passage of the Telecommunications Act of 1996 established a new regulatory framework to address the changing technological environment. This new framework provides opportunities for small and minority businesses.

- In 1993, minorities owned only 2.9 percent of all commercial broadcast radio stations.
- Currently, there is only one African American-owned telecommunications cable network operator.
- According to the National Telecommunications and Information Administration, minorities currently own only 15 out of 1,500 commercial, full-powered television stations nationwide.

Goals[111]

- Develop strategies and initiatives to provide capital for minority and small business investment in the telecommunications industry

110. Congressional Black Caucus, *The Agenda: 1997-1999*, 105th Congress of the United States, Washington, D.C., p. 8.
111. *Ibid.*

ECONOMIC TRANSFORMATION

- Expand joint venture opportunities between minority and established telecommunication companies
- Support regulatory reform to increase opportunities for minority and small business

Perspective of Telecommunications[112]

E-Rate - The CHC will continue to advocate and promote school participation in the E-rate program, which provides discounts for internal wiring and Internet connection for schools.

Computer and Technical Literacy - Promote legislation that provides funding for the training of educators on Internet and educational software learning tools. Also, it will be important to maximize the usage by low-income communities of services offered by the National Education Technology Funding Corporation.

Representation in Minority Telecommunications, Broadcasting Media - There are insufficient opportunities for Hispanic American participation in ownership. The CHC will consider financial mechanisms and the restoration of tax neutral consequences for minority acquisition. In addition, it will review appropriate tax and small business legislation to provide for equal ownership opportunity and access.

Advertising in Minority Media - A report by the FCC on the impact of advertising practices on minority broadcast stations highlighted the necessity to address corporate bias against advertising in minority media. Support increased advocacy to obtain accountability and substantiate the absence or avoidance of advertising in minority media outlets.

Low Power Radio Stations - The FCC has recently indicated that it is taking action to create a new class of low-power radio service for our local communities. This type of service is critical to our minority communities and creates a wealth of opportunities for local voices to be heard in urban neighborhoods and rural towns.

Public Interest Obligations of Broadcasters - As the industry expands, consolidates and incorporates the use of newer, advanced technologies, we must continue to enforce public interest obligations of the public airwaves. There is a need for the Caucus to be actively involved in the rule-making process as these matters evolve.

Slamming, Unfair Trade Practices/Long Distance Rates - Hispanic Americans are the largest consumers of long distance telephone services and are beholden to companies because of lack of information/lack of competition in the market to give them choices. The Federal Trade Commission should investigate business practices by telephone service providers in communities of color.

112. Congressional Hispanic Caucus, *Legislative Priorities: 1999*, 106th Congress of the United States, Washington, D.C., p. 8.

ECONOMIC TRANSFORMATION

Wealth Creation

The Million Family March supports equality of economic opportunity. All families should have equal membership in society with the best in civilized society.

The spending power of Black American, Hispanic American, Native American, Asian and Pacific Islander American and Arab American families is in the trillions of dollars annually. Yet, there have been historic and contemporary obstacles that prevented and deter accumulating real wealth for our families.

The Congressional Black Caucus maintains that "home ownership is the cornerstone of asset- building and wealth accumulation."[113] Public policies at the federal and state levels should encourage and enable families to purchase real estate.

The Million Family March is mobilizing families to become stronger financially and spiritually toward greater wealth development. On one hand we believe in self-reliance and self-sufficiency. On the other hand, we know our true economic potential can not be maximized in a vacuum or in isolation from capital.

Preparation and ongoing training programs are key factors in attempting to acquire wealth.

Action Items

- Support wealth accumulation seminars, community meetings and local campaigns.
- Promote asset development and management
- Invest in corporate-responsible companies
- Utilize information technology to enhance family and community development
- Organize investment clubs for families
- Develop joint economic business ventures that serve the development interests of the family and community

---

113. Congressional Black Caucus, *"Raising the Roof: A Southeastern Regional Summit on Housing and Wealth Accumulation,"* Charlotte, N.C., July 24, 1999.

ECONOMIC TRANSFORMATION

ECONOMIC TRANSFORMATION

Capital Formation

Create Capital to Assist Minority Business Development[114]

Access to capital is one of the most formidable barriers to creating and sustaining successful minority-owned firms.

Background

Studies have shown that, with the same training, equity, and experience, the success rate for minority companies is the same as for non-minority companies. Yet, minority firms traditionally have not had access to the capital necessary to compete and expand their businesses.

- In 1992, African Americans and other minorities, collectively, owned only 11 percent of all businesses in America.
- Annual sales receipts for minority-owned companies averaged only $202,000, compared with an average of $3.3 million for White-owned businesses.
- Annual sales receipts for businesses owned by African American men averaged only $23,688, and sales receipts for businesses owned by African American women averaged only $8,510.

Goals[115]

- Create a business development fund and other capital pools for investment in small and minority-owned businesses
- Enhance the ability of minority-focused investment entities to access private capital markets through targeted tax incentives and institutional capital providers
- Monitor the implementation of the community Reinvestment Act (CRA) to ensure its effectiveness

---

114. Congressional Black Caucus, *The Agenda: 1997-1999, 105th Congress of the United States,* *Washington, D.C., p. 10.*
115. *Ibid.*

ECONOMIC TRANSFORMATION

The District of Columbia

Revitalize Our Nation's Capital[116]

The nation's capital is in financial crisis. Limited by a restricted tax base and by Congressional oversight, the city is faced with unique obstacles to solving its problems.

Background

The District of Columbia faces a structural crisis similar to other older American cities. Over 125,000 people have left the city since 1970, drastically reducing its tax base. Firms also have created jobs in the suburbs rather than in the city. In addition, federal support for public assistance to low-income families has declined since 1970, while health care and public safety costs have risen dramatically.

The Home Rule Act of 1974, which the CBC supports, also transferred to the district, responsibilities traditionally handled by states including excessive pension liabilities. However, unlike states, the district faces a restricted tax base that prevents it from increasing its revenue sources. In 1995, this resulted in a debt crisis that caused the district to lose its ability to borrow from Wall Street. Following this loss, Congress created a financial control board, similar to boards in other troubled cities, to exercise certain oversight and management functions of the city.

Goals[117]

- Support full voting rights and representation for the citizens of the District of Columbia
- Support tax incentives and other creative proposals to reduce the exodus of jobs and the middle-class from the District of Columbia
- Challenge taxation without representation
- Full voting rights for D.C. representatives in Congress
- A more balanced federal payment in the District of Columbia

116. *Congressional Black Caucus, The Agenda: 1997-1999*, 105th Congress of the United States, Washington, D.C., p. 12.
117. *Ibid.*

Economic Transformation

ECONOMIC TRANSFORMATION

Affirmative Action

Ensure Equal Opportunity[118]

Affirmative action is being attacked in the courts, Congress, our states and our schools. If successful, women and minorities will lose many of the gains in employment, education and business opportunities they have earned over the past 30 years.

Background

Several recent Supreme Court and other federal court rulings have opened the door to the dismantling of affirmative action programs. In Adarand v. Pena in 1995, the Supreme Court made it harder to justify using federal affirmative action contracting programs. Following Adarand, legislation was introduced in Congress to end federal affirmative action programs altogether. While the CBC successfully led the effort to block the legislation in 1998, similar legislation was introduced last year.

Similarly, a federal court ruled in Hopwood v. State of Texas, that racial diversity used to remedy past discrimination was not enough of a compelling governmental interest to justify a law school affirmative action program. The universities of California, Texas, Louisiana, and Georgia either have dismantled, or are considering dismantling their affirmative action programs.

Also, in November 1996, California voters approved Proposition 209, the so-called California Civil Rights Initiative. This measure eliminates state affirmative action in education, contraction and employment. The initiative is currently being challenged. Similar ballot initiatives were attempted in Colorado, Washington, Oregon and Florida. Virtually identical bills were introduced in 15 state legislatures.

Americans for a Fair Chance (AFC) has been organized as a consortium of six legal rights groups to mobilize public and legal opinion in support of the issue of Affirmative Action.

The groups include: Committee for Civil Rights Under Law; Mexican American Legal Defense and Educational Fund; National Asian Pacific American Legal Consortium; NAACP Legal Defense and Educational Fund, Inc.; National Women's Law Center and the National Partnership for Women and Families.[119]

118. Congressional Black Caucus, *The Agenda: 1997-1999*, 105th Congress of the United States, Washington, D.C., p. 27.
119. NAPLC, Internet:www.napal.org/contact/pro_affirmative2.html.

Economic Transformation

Americans for a Fair Chance has concluded that numerous "recent examples of blatant discrimination make clear the continuing need for affirmative action."[120]

Goals[121]

- Oppose any effort to eliminate federal affirmative action programs
- Work with the administration to shape proposed affirmative action regulations, and to ensure enforcement and compliance with existing affirmative action laws
- Support efforts at the state level to defeat legislation and ballot initiatives that would dismantle affirmative action programs

120. *Ibid.*
121. *Ibid.*

ECONOMIC TRANSFORMATION

National Security

Redefine and Improve Security for All Americans[122]

It is time to redefine our notion of national security. This country now spends as much on its military budget as all the other countries of the world combined. We have the military power to defend our national interests, but we must figure out how to apply our resources and capabilities to meet our domestic national security needs and to create a more stable world.

Background

With the fall of the Berlin Wall and the break up of the Soviet Union, the implications for U.S. national security have changed fundamentally. A reassessment by Congress of our national security needs in light of these changes is long overdue. The military can no longer be seen as the only national security expenditure and the only critical element of any comprehensive national security strategy.

Foreign assistance programs that create international stability also must be seen as central to our total national security requirements. We must also make military spending decisions in light of the impact those decisions have on our ability to solve pressing domestic problems that undermine our national security. Only in this context can the federal budget finally advance the national security needs of our people.

Goals[123]

- Work to redefine the notion of national security by ensuring a healthy citizenry and a vibrant economy
- Work to solve the economic conditions that lead to war and to determine the proper size and capabilities of a well-equipped military to peace internationally

Work on economic conversion to revive communities that have relied on military programs for economic survival.

---

122. Congressional Black Caucus, *The Agenda: 1997-1999*, 105th Congress of the United States, Washington, D.C., p. 17.
123. *Ibid.*

ECONOMIC TRANSFORMATION

ECONOMIC TRANSFORMATION

INTERNATIONAL AFFAIRS

INTERNATIONAL AFFAIRS

Foreign Policy

If we measure the correctness of domestic and foreign policy using the criteria: (1) That which encourages the development of human beings along the lines of that which The Creator purposed for the human beings; (2) that which strengthens marriage; (3) that which strengthens and protects the family; then our policies, both domestic and foreign, can be considered good policies. For, any policy that is good for self can be good for others, if we love for our brother or neighbor what we love for ourselves.

Jesus laid down the two basic Commandments, which must form the basis of our thinking as we develop policies, rules, regulations and laws that affect the human condition. Jesus said the First and Greatest Commandment is, **Thou shaft love the Lord, thy God, with all thy heart, and with all thy soul, and with all thy mind.** *The Second Commandment is like unto it,* **Thou shaft love thy neighbor as thyself. On these two Commandments (of Love) hang all The Law and the Prophets.**

We have to admit that the Prophets, wherever they have appeared on the earth, have given us noble examples of human conduct. Although, the Bible lists a number of faults of many of the Prophets, the Holy Qur'an holds them sinless. However, the fact that The Law and the Prophets hang from, or are connected, to these Two Great Commandments of Love, should tell us that if this is truly a government under Allah (God), indivisible, with liberty and justice for all, then, all of the policies, domestic and foreign, must reflect these Commandments.

This is not the case. The nations of the earth have been crushed and exploited because of the policies of the powerful industrial nations of the world.

By Allah's (God's) permission, America has become the only remaining superpower and sits at the top of a unipolar world. America stands in the position of Khalifah and/or vicegerent, or that which stands in the place of Allah (God). Therefore, America, moreso than any other nation, should and must act in the place of Allah (God) who has raised her in eminence and power as no other nation in the last 6,000 years.

What should America's policies be toward all the nations of the earth?

Since America has been founded, developed, and peopled by all of the races, nations, and ethnic groups of the world, and since all of the peoples of the world who are citizens of the United States of America have contributed to her greatness and helped her to rise to the great position that she now holds, her policies, should then reflect her gratitude to all the nations of the earth for what they have given to make America.

When we look at those who helped to make America the greatest nuclear power on the earth–the scientists, the scholars, and the people who caused this to hap-

pen are practically from all the nations and races of the earth.

When we took at America's mastery of the race in space—the scientists, scholars, and the people who made this happen are from every race and practically every nation on this earth.

When we look at the advancement in science, technology, and medicine you will find that those who helped to make this happen are from every race and practically every nation on this earth.

I repeat, America's foreign policy should reflect her gratitude to the nations of the earth who have contributed their sons and daughters to raise America to the great position that she now holds.

Since America's foreign policies are driven by corporate greed; since America's relationship to the poor countries of the world allows America and the industrialized nations to take produce and raw materials from these nations, at a small price, which disallows these nations to do for their people what America and Europe have been able to do for their people, then these policies must be re-evaluated and rethought.

If leaders arise in these nations who recognize the injustice of the policies of America and Europe and seek to change the relationship with America and Europe to one that is more just and equitable, it then becomes a policy of the governments of the United States and Europe to get rid of these leaders who stand in the way of the bottom line of corporate greed. These industrialized governments even foment civil strife in these countries setting up leaders who are more favorable to America's and Europe's bottom line; these policies that disturb and destroy the abilities of countries to develop their people; these policies that promote strife which allows the merchants of death to sell weapons of war to profit from the destruction of men, women and children are not policies that reflect the love of neighbor. These unjust policies that bring war to other nations will ultimately bring a great war to the door of the United States of America.

This will cause the President of the United States of America to break into our families and summon our sons and daughters to send them off to areas of conflict that did not necessarily have to be so if America's policies were based on the Two Great Commandments that Jesus gave to the Christian world and also to all of humanity.

America owes a debt to Europe so she will always strive to have a good relationship with Europe, but America and Europe also owe a debt to Africa. Therefore, their policies must reflect the contribution that Africans have made to America's and Europe's development. Their policies toward the Caribbean, Central and South America must reflect the gratitude for that which they have added to America's greatness. America's policies toward the Middle East, Asia, the Isles of the Pacific, New Zealand and Australia should reflect the gratitude for their contributions to America's greatness.

America dislikes President Fidel Castro of Cuba, President Saddam Hussein of Iraq, President Muammar Ghadhafi of Libya, President Omar Bashir of the Sudan, President Katama of Iran, President Kim Jong Il of North Korea—all of whom have been labeled as dictators over "rogue nations" because they refuse to bow to the policies of Europe and America that will weaken their ability to serve the interests of their people, while at the same time, strengthening the bottom line of greedy multi-national corporations.

America's dislike of China is based on the same principle. The destruction of the great leaders of Africa has been because the policies of America and Europe are designed to extract the vast wealth of Africa for the good of Europe and America.

Any African leader who stands in the way of these policies must be eliminated.

Are these policies just and fair, and are they based on these Two Great Commandments of Love pronounced by Jesus?

Do these policies reflect love of thy neighbor? Of course, the answer is no. These policies reflect the inordinate self-interest and gross selfishness of America and Europe that has nothing to do with the principle of love.

Will these policies bring the best result to America and Europe in this era? Of course, the answer is no.

Since the war in Iraq ended in 1991, more Iraqis have died under sanctions than during the war. Depleted uranium was used in many of the bombs that fell on Iraq, which has affected the earth and the water and now many are dying from leukemia and other forms of cancer. If the Iraqi people had proper medication they might be able to be saved.

I ask you, is this good policy?

A blockade has been on Cuba for over 30 years because America does not like a communist nation 90 miles from her shore. What happened to the right of self-determination?

Jesus said, **Let your light so shine before men, that they may see your good works, and glorify your Father, who is in Heaven.**

If it is believed that the democracy that America offers is a great light, then, let this light shine. Surely, the Cuban people would see it, but this is not America's policy. It is to starve the Cubans; to deny them access to medicine; to cause the suffering of the Cuban people so that they might rise up to overthrow the leadership that America does not like. Is this the way you treat your neighbor?

If in American jurisprudence a man is innocent until proved guilty beyond a reasonable doubt, and this is a part of the constitutional guarantee of the citizens of America, should you not want it for others? Is it justified that because a charge is made by the United States government that two Libyan nationals are responsible for the bombing of Pan Am Flight #103 that American and United Nations sanctions should be placed against an entire country and people causing great harm to the people simply because America hates President Muammar Ghadhafi and his blocking of wealth to the bottom line of corporate greed? Do his nationals deserve due process?

As I see it, the American people must be informed so that they may help to guide their representatives and help their officials and government to be more just, and more humane in its policies. As long as the American people are denied access to information and knowledge, based on truth, that will help them to make good and just decisions, then the American people cannot form a counsel or cannot be helpful to guide their government.

Since this is supposed to be a government of, by, and for the people, then the people must be entrusted with knowledge that they might help to choose or elect better representation to guide them so that these elected officials truly represent the will of the people. Only a people knowledgeable, united, and organized can break the grip of the multi-national corporations that now hold sway over the United States government and its policies.

We must think of the Native American and what they have contributed and what they suffer. The government must ask the question, Are the policies of the government toward the Native Americans, the Blacks, the Hispanics, the Asians, and even poor Whites, aiding in the development of these Native Americans and others?

Is it strengthening their families' ability to do for self? Is it helping them to become productive citizens? If not, then all policies, foreign and domestic, must be reevaluated. It will take courage to do this. It will take the rising into consciousness of the masses of the American people that we, instead of corporate greed, will be the driving force behind America's domestic and foreign policies.

Lastly, it is our hope in the town hall discussions of this agenda that these thoughts and this criterion will be used to look at all America's policies-domestic and foreign.[124]

The following are key American foreign policy issues that will be addressed at the Million Family March:

- More U.S. investment in the development of Africa that is mutually beneficial to protect the rights of the indigenous people.
- More U.S. investment in the development of Latin America that is mutually beneficial to protect the rights of the indigenous people.
- More U.S. investment in the development of the Caribbean that is mutually beneficial to protect the rights of the indigenous people.
- Reform International Monetary Fund (IMF)
- Reform World Trade Organization (WTO).
- Support international debt forgiveness. Review of human rights violations as a result of economic sanctions, blockades and other governmental acts that threaten the stability of family life and peace in other sovereign nations.

124. *Statement from The Honorable Minister Louis Farrakhan, Convener of The Million Family March, February 5, 2000.*

INTERNATIONAL AFFAIRS

International Relations[125]

Emergency Supplemental for Central America

The funds requested by the president are critical to the reconstruction of Central America in the wake of Hurricane Mitch. In February 1999, the administration submitted to Congress an Emergency Supplemental request for $956 million to assist the region's reconstruction efforts. To date, estimates place United States assistance levels at more than $300 million in medicines, emergency shelter, food, and clothing. This additional funding would bring total assistance from the United States to over $1.2 billion. The CHC will fight to ensure that Central America receives the desperately needed funds to begin the reconstruction of the region.

Development funding for Latin America and the Caribbean

Development assistance for this region has been cut to one quarter of its level from the mid-1980's. United States funding for education, microcredit, enterprise programs, health and agricultural development are crucial to help alleviate poverty in the region. This assistance also contributes to the efforts of reducing illegal immigration and drug trafficking. The administration's request for FY2000 was $309 million, an increase of nearly $20 million from previous funding levels. The CHC will work to assure that this request is funded.

North American Development (NAD) Bank

The Community Adjustment and Investment Program (CAIP) was created to provide adjustment assistance to communities that have experienced significant job losses due to the adverse affects of the North American Free Trade Agreement (NAFTA). Those workers and communities most negatively affected by NAFTA require adequate training and technical assistance due to the fact that manufacturing and other low-skilled industries are the

125. Congressional Hispanic Caucus, *Legislative Priorities: 1999*, 106th Congress of the United States, Washington, D.C., p. 8.

INTERNATIONAL AFFAIRS

most vulnerable to trade dislocation and are industries on which many poor and Latino American communities depend. The CHC will fight to ensure that the CAIP program receives the increase in funds requested by the administration for FY2000.

Increase multi-lateral relations

The CHC will seek to strengthen ties with our Latin America counterparts. This increased interaction will provide valuable insight into current events of the region, including the growing global financial crisis, the ongoing political and economic environment throughout Latin America and the development of the free trade area of the Americas.

The Future of Native Americans in America

The Million Family March supports and respects the human rights of Native Americans. Native American families not only have a God-given right to exist free of genocide and oppression, but Native American families also have a God-given right to self-determination.

The American Indian Movement (AIM) has issued a (manifesto) list of public policy proposals, objectives and plans to clarify and advance the interests of Native Indians in America. The 21st Century should be the century in which the United States government should engage in acts of atonement, repentance, and restoration toward the Indian nations and all Native Americans.

In the "Preamble: An Indian Manifesto for Restitution, Reparations, Restoration of Lands For a Reconstruction of An Indian Future In America," the American Indian Movement affirms:

> *We need not give another recitation of past complaints nor engage in redundant dialogue of discontent. Our conditions and their cause for being should perhaps be best known by those who have written the record of America's action against Indian people. … We seek a new American majority, a majority that is not content to confirm itself by superiority in numbers, but which by conscience is committed toward prevailing upon the public will in ceasing wrongs and in doing right. For our part, in words and deeds of coming days, we propose to produce a rational, reasoned manifesto for construction of an Indian future in America. If America has maintained faith with its original spirit, or may recognize it now, we should not be denied.[126]*

Action Items[127]

- Restoration of constitutional treaty-taking authority; The President of the United States should propose to reinstate federal recognition

126. American Indian Movement (AIM), Internet: www.aimovement.org.
127. *Ibid.*

of "Indian Tribes and Nations" in a manner that respects the indigenous rights of Native Americans in regard to land, treaties and other issues of constitutional sovereignty

- Establishment of Treaty Commission to make new treaties
- Native American leadership, selected by Indian people at a future date, should be given an opportunity to address a joint session of the United States Congress
- Resume federal protective jurisdiction for offenses against Indians
- Establishment of a special commission to review past treaty commitments and violations
- Resubmission of unratified treaties to the United States Senate
- Public policy should respect self-government of Native Americans as detailed in ratified treaties between the government of the United States and the government of Indian Nations
- Support mandatory judicial and injunctive relief against treaty rights violations
- Support the creation of a Congressional joint committee on reconstruction of Indian relations
- Land reform and restoration of millions of acres of Native American lands
- Restoration of rights to Indians terminated by the enrollment and revocation of prohibitions against "dual benefits"
- Creation of an "Office of Federal Indian Relations and Community Reconstruction"
- Protection of Indians' religious freedom and cultural integrity
- Protect and secure the environmental integrity of American Indian territories

The Global Sullivan Principles[128]

The Global Sullivan Principles are a positive, aspirational framework against which the internal policies and practices of socially responsible companies, small and large, can be aligned. They are intended to be succinct (rather than detailed or highly prescriptive), understandable (by all stakeholders), and universal (rather than reflective of any particular social, cultural, or geographical tradition).

Accordingly, we will:

- Express our support for universal human rights and particularly, those of our employees, the communities within which we operate, and parties with whom we do business.
- Promote equal opportunity for our employees at all levels of the company with respect to issues such as color, race, gender, age, ethnicity or religious beliefs, and operate without unacceptable worker treatment such as the exploitation of children, physical punishment, female abuse, involuntary servitude, or other forms of abuse.
- Respect our employees' to enable them to meet at least their basic needs and provide the opportunity to improve their skill and capability in order to raise their social and economic opportunities.
- Provide fair competition including respect for intellectual and other property rights, and not offer, pay or accept bribes.
- Work with governments and communities in which we do business to improve the quality of life in those communities, their educational, cultural, economic and social well-being and seek to provide training and opportunities for workers from disadvantaged backgrounds.
- Promote the application of these principles by those with whom we do business.

We will be transparent in our implementation of these principles and provide information which demonstrates publicly our commitment to them.

INTERNATIONAL AFFAIRS

---

128. The Reverend Leon H. Sullivan, *The Global Sullivan Principles*, International Foundation for Education and Self-Help, 1999 Phoenix, Arizona, p. 2.

Expand Assistance and Support for Africa and the Caribbean[129]

The United States must rethink its policy towards Africa and the Caribbean. Its unstated policy of economic and political marginalization of these regions ignores their importance and impedes their stability, democratization and broad-based economic growth.

Background

Over the past decade, the United States has significantly decreased its economic commitment to Africa and the Caribbean. According to experts, while U.S., foreign aid has generally decreased, Africa and the Caribbean have taken a disproportionate share of the cuts.

- The Africa Development Fund is currently under funded.
- The Gross National Product (GNP) per capita earnings for Africa is only $617 and just $490 for Sub-Saharan Africa.

In addition, a recent World Trade Organization (WTO) ruling, initiated by the U.S., will devastate the economy of many Caribbean banana-producing countries. As much as 70 percent of the total export revenues of some Caribbean countries come from banana exports.

Goals[130]

- Protect and expand U.S. foreign assistance to Africa and the Caribbean
- Support peace, stability, and freedom, and promote democracy and development in all African countries
- Seek consensus building, adequate United Nations (UN) reform, and support for the UN and its special agencies and regional organizations such as the Organization of African Unity

129. Congressional Black Caucus, *The Agenda: 1997-1999*, 105th Congress of the United States, Washington, D.C., p. 13.
130. *Ibid.*

INTERNATIONAL AFFAIRS

- Negotiate an equitable settlement of the WTO Caribbean banana dispute to provide economic stability for the region
- Address Virgin Island territorial issues
- Support efforts to end genocide and slavery and seek stability and justice for refugees everywhere

Acknowledgements

The Million Family March is very grateful for the contributions to the following persons who served on the Drafting Committee of The National Agenda:

Leonard G. Dunston, Rosaline Preudhomme, Spike Moss, Sheron Thompson-Moss, Osohar Berry, Reverend and Mrs. Zakery Oliver, Rose Sanders, Malika Sanders, Rudolph Stewart III, Erica Bennett, Marion Barry, Cora Masters Barry, Chuck Hicks, Marcia Griffin, Claudette Marie Muhammad, Lydia Muhammad, A. Arif Muhammad, Ruth Muhammad, Dr. William Ridgely, Barry Crumley, A. Khadir Muhammad, Muhammad Abdulah Muhammad, Askia Muhammad, Jackie Muhammad, Carole Harper, Barbara Muhammad, Brenda Muhammad, Charlene Muhammad, Mary Ellen Salaam Muhammad, Rahim Jenkins, Mark Thompson, Yalanda Muhammad, Zaheer Ali Muhammad, Jonathan Gullery, Kay Brausen and numerous others.

We are also thankful for the tireless efforts of the staff assigned to the task of completing The National Agenda:

Samiyyah Muhammad, Sharien Muhammad, Karen Muhammad, Corey Muhammad, Drayton Muhammad, Khalidah Muhammad, Debra Khaliq Muhammad, Nafeesa Muhammad, Martha R. Muhammad, Saffiyyah Muhammad, Kim Muhammad and Alethea Muhammad.

A Special thanks to: Dr. Dorothy Height, Dr. Jane Smith and the National Council of Negro Women.

Finally, the help of scholars from various academic and theological disciplines was invaluable, and we acknowledge:

Manning Marable, Cornell West, Andrew Wilson, James Taylor, Frank Kaufman, Michael Mickler, Theodore Shimyo, Ronald Walters, Maulana Karenga, Joong Hyun Pak, Vernon Bellecourt and Jim Zogby.

We appreciate the guidance and support from the Chief of Staff, Brother Leonard F. Muhammad and the National Board of Laborers.

We are all ultimately grateful and thankful to Allah (God) for the call of the Million Family March through the Honorable Minister Louis Farrakhan. The publication of The National Agenda has been a labor of love and respect for humanity. May Allah bless all of us with success.

Minister Benjamin F. Muhammad
Editor

INTERNATIONAL AFFAIRS